Christopher Faulkner / Paul Duncan (Ed.)

JEAN RENOIR

A Conversation with His Films 1894–1979

TASCHEN

HONG KONG KÖLN LONDON LOS ANGELES MADRID PARIS TOKYO

FRONT COVER
Still from 'Toni' (1935)
In one of the film's few close-ups, Joséfa cradles
the gun with which she is about to shoot husband
Albert for having brutalized her once too often.

FIRST PAGE
Still from 'French Cancan' (1955)
The cancan dancers rehearse their routine at
Madame Guibole's dance studio in preparation
for the grand opening of the Moulin Rouge.

FRONTISPIECE
Jean Renoir
Behind the easy manner and light touch, few
people saw Renoir's intensity.

THIS PAGE
1 On the set of 'Swamp Water' (1941)
During a break on location at the Okefenokee
Swamp in Georgia, Renoir looks over the
shooting script with Anne Baxter and Dana
Andrews.

2 On the set of 'The Golden Coach' (1954)
Renoir is in serious discussion with his
temperamental star, Anna Magnani, about the
part of Camilla.

OPPOSITE
1 On the set of 'La Grande Illusion' (1937)
The cast of prisoners of war, their guards and a
few extras gather for the customary group
photograph at the conclusion of shooting. As
usual, Renoir is part of the crowd.
2 Michel Simon and Jean Renoir
The actor Michel Simon and Renoir share a
laugh during the program 'Cinéastes de notre
temps' as they reminisce about working together
in the late 1920s and early 1930s.

BACK COVER
Jean Renoir in New York (1956)
Renoir sticks his head out a window in New York
to catch a view of the city. The Chrysler Building
is in the background.

To stay informed about upcoming TASCHEN titles, please request our magazine at
www.taschen.com/magazine or write to TASCHEN America, 6671 Sunset Boulevard, Suite
1508, USA-Los Angeles, CA 90028, contact-us@taschen.com, Fax: +1-323-463.4442.
We will be happy to send you a free copy of our magazine which is filled with information
about all of our books.

© 2007 TASCHEN GmbH
Hohenzollernring 53, D–50672 Köln
www.taschen.com

Editor/Picture Research/Layout: Paul Duncan/Wordsmith Solutions
Editorial Coordination: Martin Holz, Cologne
Production Coordination: Martina Ciborowius, Cologne
Typeface Design: Sense/Net, Andy Disl, Cologne
Printed in China
ISBN 978-3-8228-3097-0

Notes
A superscript number indicates a reference to a note on page 192

Images
Jean Renoir Collection, UCLA, Los Angeles: 1, 8, 10, 11, 12, 13 (2), 14
(2), 15 (2), 16, 42/43, 44, 45 (2), 47, 48, 49, 55, 64 (2), 73, 74, 81,
82/83, 84, 93, 98, 101, 106, 107, 110, 112 (2), 113, 114, 115, 116
(2), 118, 121, 126, 136, 141, 143, 151, 152, 153, 155 (2), 162, 163,
172 (2), 178 (2), 179 (2), 180, 181, 184 (3), 185, Back Cover
BiFi, Paris: 5, 20, 22, 23 (2), 25, 26, 27, 28, 29, 31, 32/33, 36 (2), 39 (2),
40, 41 (2), 46, 47, 54, 56, 57, 58 (2), 61, 62, 70, 76, 77, 78/79, 80,
81, 84, 86, 87, 88, 95, 96 (2), 97, 99 (2), 102, 103, 104/105, 106 (2),
107 (2), 121, 138, 141, 146 (2), 148, 152, 153, 154/155, 170, 172,
173, 174, 175, 176, 185
British Film Institute Stills, Posters and Designs, London: 30, 34/35, 35 (2),
42, 50, 52 (2), 53, 59, 66, 68, 69, 71, 72 (2), 76, 85, 88, 89, 90, 93
(2), 100, 120 (2), 121, 124, 125, 128, 131, 134, 142, 147, 149, 150,
171 (2), 177
Photofest, New York: 2, 4, 21, 25 (2), 46, 47, 63, 68, 69, 70, 75, 77, 80,
90, 94, 114, 115, 118, 119, 120, 128, 130, 132, 133, 134, 135, 156
(2), 171, 177
The Kobal Collection, London/New York: Cover, 32, 50 (2), 55, 66, 67, 74,
120, 124, 126, 127, 140, 157
Everett Collection, New York: 14, 64, 117, 133, 144 (2), 145 (2)
Joel Finler Collection, London: 38, 129, 130, 138, 139 (2), 150 (2)
Magnum Photos/Agentur Focus: Henri Cartier-Bresson 5; Robert Capa
149; René Burri 158/159, 160 (2)
Paris-Match, Paris: Jack Garofalo 164/165, 166/167, IZIS 168/169
CORBIS: Studio Patellani 108/109, Douglas Kirkland 182/183
Pierre-Auguste Renoir: 6, 9, 10

Introduction

Renoir liked to tell the story that when he came into the world his father roared that his mouth gaped like a furnace. The merit of this story is that it draws attention to two of Jean's principal attributes, both of which bear on his practice as one of the world's greatest film-makers: his love of food and his love of conversation. Renoir's personal fondness for the table is well known and has been reliably reported by many of his friends and colleagues. For Renoir a certain *douceur de vivre* was synonymous with food. He distrusted preparation that was too elaborate and meals that were too formal. He preferred a healthy *pot au feu*, an unpretentious sandwich, or an easy omelette, and heartily approved of regional dishes (see his films *Toni* and *La Marseillaise*, for example). *Renoir, My Father*, his biography of Pierre-Auguste, includes his mother's recipe for chicken *sauté*. Renoir's films are splendid with gastronomic moments. In Renoir's universe, one negotiates the world through one's palate and taste, as much as one does through one's eye and sight. Food, the judgements made of it, the discourse about it, is one of the most important motifs through all his work. The production, circulation and exchange of food inform social relations. What one eats or how one cooks may be a sign of moral, political, or cultural authority. Food and drink shared between characters (in *La Bête humaine*, say), or shared across classes and between nationalities (in *La Grande Illusion*) lead to camaraderie and good conversation.

The many occasions in Renoir's films devoted to the preparation and consumption of food are what the Russian literary historian Mikhail Bakhtin would call a chronotope. A chronotope is an interdependent time-space, charged with emotions and values,' 'the place where the knots of narrative are tied and untied.'[1] In these respects, a chronotope is something more than a motif. This is where narrative and meaning are made concrete and where the real historical, social world is most in evidence.

If many of Renoir's films include a scene of conversation around a dinner table, this is because he thought of one's engagement with the world, with others, and with the arts to be like an ongoing conversation. To sit down before a film by Renoir is to enter into conversation with the film-maker through his work. This conversation may be quiet or shrill, frustrating or enlightening, but it will rarely be dull. Even the making of his films seems to have been like a conversation between all those involved, as so many of his actors and crew members have warmly testified in

'Jean Renoir as a Hunter' (1910)
Pierre-Auguste's magnificent painting of Jean as 'Le Chasseur' ('The Hunter'), a work which now hangs in the Los Angeles County Museum of Art. Ironically, Jean could not hurt a fly and was known to pick up spiders in his house and return them to the garden.

'Among seekers of truth, painters perhaps come closest to discovering the secret of the balance of forces in the universe, and hence of man's fulfilment. That is why they are so important in modern life. I mean real painters, the great ones. They spring up in little groups in periods of high civilisation... The authentic, the really great, pierce through the outward appearance of things. The problem is a very simple one, that of giving back to man his earthly paradise.'

Jean Renoir

OPPOSITE
Jean Renoir
Aline, Jean's mother, his younger brother Claude ('Coco'), and his father, whose hands are already crippled with arthritis.

ABOVE
'Child with Toys (Gabrielle and Jean)' (1895-1896)
Gabrielle distracts Jean with some homemade toys so that Pierre-Auguste can paint this study of nurse and child.

ABOVE
'Jean Drawing' (1901)
This is a study in concentration as Jean bends
over his own drawing while his father captures
him at work.

RIGHT
Jean Renoir
Jean stands in a village street, probably in
Essoyes, at about the age of twelve or thirteen
already aware of the camera's presence.

Jean Renoir (1907)
Young Jean in his early teens poses in his father's studio sometime before the First World War. He is dreaming of 'The Three Musketeers' and becoming a man of honour.

'It was his belief that you should never tempt fate: "One is merely a cork," he said. "You must let yourself go along in life like a cork in the current of a stream."'

Jean Renoir

'The event which most greatly influenced the
Frenchmen of my generation was the First World
War. It is doubtful whether Western civilisation
will survive its present madness, but if our species
does not wholly disappear, and if historians still
exist a few centuries hence, they will be able to
divide the chronicle of our time into two stages –
before and after 1914.'

Jean Renoir

their memoirs and in interviews. Renoir took pride in working collaboratively. By
extension, then, Renoir has an extraordinary talent for endowing his characters with
an autonomous life. Film historians usually represent this talent by quoting the
famous line spoken by Octave (played by Renoir) in his 1939 film *La Règle du jeu*, to
the effect that "Everyone has his reasons." This does not means that all these
"reasons" that characters have for doing what they do are to be approved, but at
least they are to be acknowledged and understood. Who we are and what we do,
for good or ill, issues out of our lifelong dialogue with our fellow creatures.

Jean Renoir was born in Paris on 15 September 1894, to Pierre-Auguste Renoir, a
native of Limoges, and to Aline Charigot, a seamstress from Burgundy. Jean was
born in a house known as the Château des Brouillards, an 18th-century folly, not a
real château, which still stands in Montmartre at the bottom of rue de l'Abreuvoir
where it meets rue Girardon. By the date of Jean's birth, his father was already a
celebrated painter of the Impressionist school and through the Renoir household
passed many of the great artists and authors of the day, from Paul Cézanne to Emile
Zola.

Pierre-Auguste soon made his young son the subject of innumerable paintings. In
later life, Jean recorded his impatience at being asked to sit still and hold a pose. But
most of all he remembered his frustration at being mistaken for a girl because his
father would not permit his long, golden hair to be cut. Jean once wrote: 'I have
spent my life trying to determine the extent of my father's influence upon me,
passing over periods when I did my utmost to escape from it to dwell upon those
when my mind was filled with the precepts I thought I had gleaned from him.'[2]
Jean's lifelong predilection for working on location and for *plein air* settings,
consistent with an emphasis on the formative role of environment in shaping
personality, owe something to his father's choice of subjects and to his practice as a
painter. The evocation of his father's paintings and those of his contemporaries is
deliberate in Jean's great colour films of the 1950s and informs the themes of these
late films. In one way or another, *The River*, *The Golden Coach*, *French Cancan* and
Elena and Her Men are about art and artists and about the relationship between life
and spectacle (theatre, story, dance, painting, film).

Jean grew up in a household dominated by women, most of whom were his
father's models. Apart from his mother, the most important woman in Jean's life
was Gabrielle Renard, his mother's cousin, who was brought to Paris from the same
Burgundy village of Essoyes to be his nurse and childhood companion. Gabrielle
introduced young Jean to the French tradition of Grand Guignol, to the marionette
theatre, to the melodramas at the Théâtre Montmartre, and to his first (terrifying)
experience of cinema: 'Certainly, it was she who influenced me most of all... She
taught me to realize that the very unreality of those entertainments was a reason for
examining real life. She taught me to see the face behind the mask, and the fraud
behind the flourishes. She taught me to detest the cliché.'[3] Jean's mother died of
complications from diabetes in 1915 and thereafter Gabrielle to some extent took
her place. When Jean and Dido, his second wife, bought a house in Beverly Hills
after the Second World War, Gabrielle and her husband came from France and
bought the house next door. Renoir's autobiography, *My Life and My Films* (1974),
closes with his memory of Gabrielle and a final plea: 'Wait for me, Gabrielle.'

Jean had no formal training as a film-maker and only became a devoted cinéphile
when he discovered the films of Chaplin and sensational serials like *The Mysteries of*

Jean Renoir (1913)
Jean adopts a haughty pose in the full dress
uniform of the Chasseurs Alpins, sword and all,
at the beginning of World War One.

New York while on a leave during the First World War. After the war he tried ceramics for a while with his new wife Andrée Heuschling, but both of them spent so much time at the movies that Jean decided to try his hand at film-making so that his wife could become a star in the fashion of Lillian Gish or Mae Murray. Andrée Heuschling therefore changed her name to the more cinematic Catherine Hessling. She appears in seven of his nine silent films and stars in six of them. Renoir and Catherine admired American film-makers like D.W. Griffith and Erich von Stroheim. Renoir claimed to have seen the latter's *Foolish Wives* ten times. Renoir's first two films, *Catherine* and *La Fille de l'eau*, both made in 1924, were fairly amateur efforts made with friends in which he tried 'to reach the audience through the projection of authentic images in the tradition of French realism.'[4] With his third film, *Nana* (1926), an ambitious, expensive film adapted from the novel by Zola, Jean became a professional film-maker. Through the remainder of the 1920s he made both avant-garde and commissioned works.

Renoir was fond of saying that one starts with the environment to arrive at the self: '...man is shaped by the soil that nourishes him, by the living conditions that fashion his body and his mind, by the countryside that parades before his eyes day in and day out... a Frenchman, living in France, drinking red wine and eating Brie cheese against grey Parisian vistas, can only create a work of merit if he draws on the traditions of people who have lived as he has.'[5] This conviction helps to explain why Renoir became politically active during the 1930s and why he made films which were committed to social change.

Early on in his career Renoir endeavoured to find ways to communicate a sense of place in the cinema and to situate his characters in their environments. In time, he perfected the long take, shots of unusually long duration, accompanied by a liberal use of camera movement, through panning, dollying and tracking. He also chose lenses which would give him great depth of field, so that one could see action going on simultaneously in the foreground, middle ground and background of the shot. When these camera effects are frequently used to shoot through doors and windows and bring together an inside with an outside, we have the chronotope of the threshold. These are the times and spaces where a crisis or a break occurs in a character's life. These technical and stylistic means permitted Renoir's actors more uninterrupted playing time and enabled him to situate them in their defining milieux. 'The more I work, the more I abandon confrontations between two actors neatly set up before the camera, as in a photographer's studio. I prefer to place my characters more freely, at different distances from the camera, and to make them move.'[6] Character and space acquire a social and historical specificity. In his films of the 1930s, Renoir preferred to record sound effects directly on location and wherever possible used music that originated in the story world of the film instead of adding it later in the studio. Not surprisingly, he chose contemporary stories or stories that lent themselves to the creation of an illusion of everyday reality.

Despite this penchant for realism, there is an equally strong pull in Renoir's work toward artifice and the theatrical. This pull is there from the beginning and lasts throughout his career, with sometimes life and sometimes the theatrical temporarily in the ascendant. These tendencies are not so much in opposition as in productive tension throughout his work. There are other tensions in Renoir's work, such as those between truth and falsehood, love and friendship, nature and culture, passion and reason, performance and authenticity, reality and appearance, accident and design, and so on. Even in his practice as a film-maker on location or on the set

Jean Renoir (1916)
Top: Jean can be seen at the controls of his wood-framed Caudron biplane during the period of the Great War.
Bottom: Renoir is seated at the controls in his officer's uniform of the French Flying Corps. Aviators will figure as major characters in 'Grand Illusion' and 'The Rules of the Game'.

ABOVE
Home of Paul Cézanne, Jr. (1916)
On leave in his flyer's uniform, Jean (right) poses
for an intimate photograph with close friend Paul
Cézanne, Jr. (centre) and Georges Rivière, friend
and biographer of Pierre-Auguste Renoir. They
are with Paul's children.

RIGHT
Jean & Pierre-Auguste Renoir (c1915/1916)
Jean convalescing from his leg wound and
gathering the stories of his father's early days
that would appear in 'Renoir, My Father'.

there is a tension between planning and improvisation. In sum, much of the richness of Renoir's work, and why it continues to exercise such fascination, is because he is actually a very contradictory film-maker in whom apparent opposites are never easily resolved. Renoir is rarely comfortable with the either/or choice and much prefers the challenge of the both/and condition. That is a way of avoiding the dreaded cliché. Renoir's films offer us a world which is interpretively complex, in which it is not always easy to gauge what is right and what is wrong, in which meaning and intention may in fact be tentative, provisional, or ultimately undeterminable. Needless to say, this makes for a rich, inexhaustible conversation to which one returns again and again.

ABOVE
Jean Renoir (c1920)

LEFT
Jean Renoir
Jean examines some of his own accomplished handiwork as a ceramist that he did in the early 1920s.

The Silent Films
1924–1929

On his own account in *My Life and My Films*, the years between 1924 and 1929 were a period of discovery for Renoir. He cut his teeth on available technologies and tried out different story types. During those years, Renoir re-invented what the cinema had already accomplished technically and stylistically and attempted a few innovations of his own. Parallel editing, in-camera dissolves and superimpositions, animation, elaborate moving camera shots, time-lapse photography, slow and fast motion, the use of miniatures, matte shots, back projection and dream sequences were all part of the arsenal of techniques with which Renoir experimented in the nine films he directed during this period.

What this fascination with optical effects tells us is that the relationship of Renoir's films of the 1920s with the reality they purport to represent is highly mediated. At times, the aesthetics of cinema may seem so privileged that the subject-matter of the films recedes into the background. Narrative is at the service of style. If, as critics have often remarked, a certain tension between appearance and reality, theatre and life informs the whole of Renoir's career, in his silent period the emphasis tends to fall on the side of illusion-making and the theatrical nature of experience.

This is true from his very first film, *Catherine* (also known as *Une vie sans joie*, 1924/1927), in which the story material and narrative organisation are heavily indebted, even self-consciously indebted, to D.W. Griffith. Written and produced by Renoir, but directed with Albert Dieudonné (who would later play Napoleon for Abel Gance), *Catherine* was devised so that Catherine Hessling could play a beleaguered innocent in the style of Lillian Gish or Pearl White. She is a maid in the household of Georges and Edith Mallet in Varance, a small provincial town in the south of France. Georges, the mayor and regional deputy, has known Catherine since she was a child and treats her kindly. On the other hand, Edith, Georges' wife, carries on an affair with a monocled sub-prefect played by Renoir and treats Catherine badly. The melodramatics of the plot involve Catherine being banished first from the Mallet household for embarrassing Edith at a pretentious, local cultural event, and then from the hypocritical community who suspect her of being a prostitute. (The film's satire of the provincial bourgeoisie already anticipates *The Rules of the Game* and *The Diary of a Chambermaid*.) Catherine takes refuge from the rain overnight in a tram on a siding high on the *corniche*. Through mischance,

On the set of 'Nana' (1926)
Jean strikes a pose during the filming of 'Nana', leaning on the silent film director's telltale megaphone used for commanding attention on the set.

'I must insist on the fact that I set foot in the world of the cinema only in order to make my wife a star, intending, once this was done to return to my pottery studio. I did not foresee that once I had been caught in the machinery I should never be able to escape.'

Jean Renoir

she finds herself hurtling toward certain death on the runaway tram until she is rescued at the last minute by Georges Mallet. The entire penultimate sequence depends for its excitement upon combining superimpositions of Catherine's face and the rushing landscape with frantic cross-cutting between the would-be rescuers and the driverless tram. In one of those much older man/much younger woman pairings so familiar to French cinema, the film's unlikely conclusion finds Georges and Catherine leaving behind political ambition and reputation, differences of age and social standing, for a life together in some elsewhere. At this point in Renoir's career, any utopian prospects for the poor and dispossessed only exist as wish-fulfilling fantasy.

One comes away from *Catherine* with the impression that the stylistic means at work sometimes seem more important than the ends achieved. In a stylistically noteworthy sequence set in Nice, Catherine's 'dance of death' with Georges' nephew (he collapses and dies, perhaps in sexual ecstasy) is intercut both with shots of the room turning against the direction of the dancers and with grotesque figures from the carnival. However, beyond the spectacular montage effects in *Catherine*, also worth noticing are the naturalistic location shots of the south of France on the *corniche*, the viaduct at Grasse and the landscape around Saint-Paul-de-Vence, along with some atmospheric exteriors of Marseilles and Cagnes-sur-mer (which stands in for Varance).

The release of *Catherine* was delayed until 1927 (when it appeared as *Une vie sans joie*) because of a lawsuit between Renoir and Dieudonné over control of the film. In a contract dated 10 December 1926 (held in the Renoir Collection at UCLA), Dieudonné was designated the film's sole director and was given the exclusive authority to edit the film and to shoot any supplementary material. Pierre Braunberger was awarded world distribution rights and the right to change the title (which he evidently did). In short, Renoir lost control of his very first film, and not for the last time in his career his work appeared in a form which he had not intended.

An orphaned waif. A lecherous uncle. A poacher. A gypsy caravan. A vigilante mob. A saviour on a white horse. Such are the rather banal story materials that make up *La Fille de l'eau* (*The Whirlpool of Fate*), this time wholly directed by Renoir in the summer of 1924. Catherine Hessling is once again a hapless innocent (appropriately named Virginie), who becomes a slave to her lecherous Uncle Jeff on their working barge when her father falls overboard and drowns. She flees the clutches of dissipated Uncle Jeff to be taken in by 'the Ferret', a young poacher of the fields and streams. (No doubt Renoir was remembering his own boyhood in the Bourgogne with the poacher Godefer, as recounted years later in his autobiography.) The Ferret lives with his fortune-telling, pipe-smoking mother in a caravan on the edge of the woods. Virginie earns her keep by doing chores, while the Ferret teaches her the secrets of his trade. In retaliation for the destruction of his traps, the Ferret burns the hayricks of Justin Crépoix, a rich farmer. Crépoix assembles a drunken mob to set fire to the gypsy caravan. Virginie is once again left to fend for herself. After a severe fall, she suffers a temporary derangement which induces terrible dreams. She imagines herself being persecuted by both Uncle Jeff and farmer Crépoix. Rescue arrives in the form of Georges Raynal, son of a local landowner, who nurses Virginie back to health and employs her on his property. Following additional trials and misunderstandings, young Georges has a triumphant showdown with Jeff. Georges, his parents, and Virginie leave for Algeria. Neither differences of social class nor the colonial enterprise are obstacles to the happy union of Virginie and Georges.

If, on his own admission, Renoir thought the scenario of *La Fille de l'eau* naïve, he nevertheless took something from the exercise: 'The only benefit I derived from these first naïve works was a fairly good knowledge of the use of the camera, of lighting, of set design, and above all of special effects. I became skilled at making models: constructing a landscape to scale or a miniature street was a real pleasure for me.'[7] Indeed, one can sense that Renoir is trying to unchain the camera in the film's hesitant pans and tracks, especially in shots of the barge from the banks of the canal. A scene in which Jeff assaults Virginie in the cabin of the barge is rapidly edited with extreme close-ups at acute angles in the manner of French Impressionist film-makers of the day, such as Louis Delluc. But the most memorable sequence is Virginie's fever-induced dream of her persecution by Jeff and Crépoix and rescue by Georges. Renoir uses superimpositions, negative images, slow-motion, stop-action, miniatures and an impressive shot of Georges carrying Virginie away on his white horse. This latter effect was achieved by filming horse and riders against a huge, revolving cylinder, and then superimposing them over images of the unrolling landscape and sky. The sequence concludes with Virginie's long fall from the horse through empty space. This dream sequence was excerpted and shown as a self-contained film to avant-garde audiences at the Théâtre Vieux-Colombier. *La Fille de l'eau* also has some remarkable naturalistic views of the forest, the fields, the canal and the Loing River in and around Fontainebleau where the film was shot. This was Jean's first collaboration with his older brother Pierre, who appears here in the sequence of the burning of the caravan as a menacing peasant with a pitchfork.

The lack of any commercial or critical success for his first two films led Renoir to doubt his talents as a film-maker. He even tried his hand at opening an art gallery in Paris. However, this waywardness did not last, and the film-making bug bit once more. *Nana*, adapted from the Zola novel, was the next project, an ambitious one, and sufficiently expensive that Renoir was forced to sell many of his father's paintings that had come to him as his inheritance to cover the production costs. This was a necessity that clearly troubled him. It was not until after the Second World War that he was able to buy back Pierre-Auguste's *Le Chasseur*, the famous painting of Jean dressed as a young hunter that now hangs in the Los Angeles County Museum of Art, courtesy of a donation from his son, Alain.

Nana was a French-German co-production that took almost five months to make and cost well over 1,000,000 francs. It had its Paris premiere in April 1926 at the Moulin Rouge (fitting enough, since there is a memorable scene of the performance of the cancan). Renoir remembered an audience divided between avant-garde admirers and mainstream antagonists: 'The film ran to an accompaniment of whistles and catcalls punctuated with bursts of hearty applause.'[8] This was an important and ambitious film at this early stage in Renoir's career, even if it did not turn out to be the success he had hoped. Catherine Hessling stars as the lubricious Nana, who gets what she wants by spreading her thighs for *le tout Paris*, both on and off the stage. She is meant to be the type of the devouring woman who turns men helpless before her physical charms. However, one of the serious problems with *Nana* is that Catherine Hessling in the title role is too doll-like and not sensual enough to persuade the spectator of her universal allure. Renoir himself referred to her as a 'marionette'. Her contorted facial expressions, her winks and grimaces, and her exaggerated gestures make her the type of the *femme enfant*

BELOW
Still from 'Catherine' (1924)
In the course of fleeing the Mallet household, Catherine pauses by the roadway along the corniche and gives us a glimpse of a Provençal village spread out behind her.

BOTTOM
Still from 'Catherine' (1924)
In the film's penultimate sequence, Catherine is trapped on the driverless, runaway tram as it hurtles toward the cliff edge.

ABOVE
On the set of 'La Fille de l'eau' (1925)
The camera teeters awkwardly on the edge of the
barge on a canal near Fontainebleau to get a
shot of Pierre Lestringuez as lecherous Uncle
Jeff.

OPPOSITE
Still from 'La Fille de l'eau' (1925)
Virginie (Catherine Hessling) clutches at some
loose gravel as she struggles to make her way up
the edge of a cliff.

rather than the mature figure of ravenous sexual appetite that the source material demands. Because this is supposed to be a narrative driven by male desire for the sexualised female body, it is therefore difficult to accept that Count Muffat would become instantly besotted by her, or that her other suitors, the Count de Vandeuvres and his nephew Georges, would easily succumb to the same obsessive passion.

Nana is presumed to solicit male desire by her calculated exhibitionism. In a medium, film, which is perfectly suited to conveying the arousal of male desire through the gaze at the female body, Catherine Hessling's appearance and acting style are thus something of a drawback. Appropriately enough, the film begins with Nana making a spectacle of herself on stage within an operatic spectacle called 'The Blonde Venus'. As she is lowered to the stage for her grand entrance, the stage machinery goes awry and Nana is left airily suspended above the floor in a mockery of her much-vaunted corporeality. Completely without dignity, vulgar, atrocious, Nana breaks with her role and engages the audience, in particular the star-struck Muffat. Muffat buys Nana a part she covets in a forthcoming production known, ironically, as 'La Petite duchesse' ('The Little Duchess'). By bankrolling the theatre, Muffat establishes the economy of sex and money which will drive Nana's ambition. The story of Nana, the prostitute, foregrounds the commodification of sexuality and the sexualisation of the commodity in late 19th-century French society (and in the early 20th, for that matter).

When Nana gives up the theatre and becomes a professional courtesan, she takes on a role different in degree but not in kind from the one she has left. She can force tears when necessary or get Muffat to perform like a pet dog. We are introduced to her new lifestyle in a scene which begins with a close-up of a cupid-like figure on the headboard of her bed. The camera then tilts down and pulls back to reveal an enormous bed heaped with gifts and purchases. (This camera movement, extending from close-up to long shot, will become a signature Renoir effect in future work.) In a later scene, Vandeuvres imagines Nana lying on this same bed as she runs showers of gold coins through her fingers. Everything about Nana's townhouse is oversize, including its salon and its grand staircase, presumably to convey something of her sexual appetite and its power to command so much male attention. Vandeuvres is said to be "perverted", morally and sexually, by his contact with Nana. His attempt to fix the outcome of the Grand Prix by favouring his racehorse Nana is exposed. Broken, dishonoured, rejected by Nana, he takes poison and, in a scene of great cruelty, sets fire to his stable with his prize horse Nana inside. However, when Georges commits suicide in her townhouse, Nana begins to come undone. Her servants rob her and fall into debauchery. She endeavours to escape her ghosts by living it up at the Bal Mabille and even joining in the cancan. However, Nana's sexuality, this perversion, has become self-corrupting. She is discovered to have smallpox. Muffat goes to her one last time and watches her die in the bed that made and unmade both her reputation and her fortune.

Nana takes her lovers from the upper classes, who install her in a Paris townhouse and ply her with expensive gifts in exchange for her sexual favours. Unfortunately, despite the contrast between Nana's class origins and those of her suitors, the film (unlike the novel), does not really explore the potential for a social critique of upper-class hypocrisy about women and/or their sexuality. The comparison in the film of Nana to a 'mouche d'or' ('a golden fly') does not really explain that this metaphor is meant to communicate the contagion she spreads by

TOP
Still from 'La Fille de l'eau' (1925)
In Virginie's dream, Uncle Jeff hangs ominously against a tree trunk. This dream sequence was shown in avant-garde circles independently of the full-length film.

ABOVE
Still from 'La Fille de l'eau' (1925)
In the night-ride in her dream, Catherine is spirited away by Georges (Harold Livingston) on his white charger, only for her to slip from the horse and fall through the sky.

OPPOSITE
On the set of 'La Fille de l'eau' (1925)
Against a specially contrived revolving cylinder as backdrop, preparations are made to shoot the night-ride from Catherine's dream sequence. The shot will be superimposed over images of clouds and sky.

way of the condensation of sex and money on her working-class body.[9] *Nana* is also a meant to be a story of modern, urban life, a story of Paris as 'capital' of the 19th century, in Walter Benjamin's famous formulation. Such an insight offers all sorts of potential for class analysis. However, despite its ambition, the film seems to have missed numerous opportunities for a more searching and complex treatment of its very interesting subject-matter.

The commercial disaster of *Nana* did lead to one of Renoir's most interesting films of the silent period. *Sur un air de Charleston* (*Charleston*) was made in a few days in the fall of 1926 from the metres of film left over after shooting *Nana*. Once again Renoir brought in his friends, but this time added Johnny Hudgins to the mix, the accomplished dancer and comedian from the celebrated Revue Nègre that stormed Paris in 1925 and made Josephine Baker a star. Together Hudgins and Renoir made a clever and engaging film about a black explorer who comes by spaceship from the advanced civilisation of Africa to the 'Unknown Lands' of Europe, which have apparently been devastated by some sort of apocalyptic event. Amidst the wreckage of a Paris street, he meets a local white savage (Catherine Hessling), who communicates with him by teaching him to dance the Charleston. The performance is erotic, and thus a dance of courtship, as well as exotic, which makes the girl an anthropological curiosity. At the end, she is spirited away in the explorer's space ship, evidently a willing captive. The film should not be regarded as merely a fanciful exercise designed to showcase the contemporary mania for the Charleston introduced to France by Josephine Baker the year before. Instead, through its inversion of racial stereotypes and clichés the film becomes a satire of the white, European exoticization of black performers, of primitivism as a (demeaning) discourse about black culture, and of the tendency to collapse the difference between black Africans and black Americans.

Nothing remains of *Marquitta*, the film that Renoir made in the winter of 1927. Apart from a few stills, our knowledge of the film depends upon contemporary reviews and a synopsis of the film which appeared in *Cinémagazine*.[10] By this account, Marquitta, the heroine of the story, is a street-singer who is discovered performing in the working-class area of La Villette, in Paris, by an eastern European Prince. He falls in love with her and takes her to his palace on the Riviera, where he acts as Pygmalion to her Galatea. All does not go well, because the Prince accuses Marquitta of stealing a sapphire and throws her back onto the street. However, their fortunes are reversed when Marquitta becomes a great star and the Prince loses his fortune in a revolution and turns to singing on the street himself. Now she takes him in, briefly, but throws him out in his turn when he flies into a rage as she attempts to return his lost sapphire. The film concludes with their reconciliation after an automobile chase along the *corniche* thwarts the Prince's attempted suicide. Renoir evidently regarded the film as a job of work, but it did earn praise for its actors, for its location work in Paris and on the Côte d'Azur, for its camera work ('Les angles de prises de vues sont toujours excellents, parfois originaux'/'The camera set-ups are always excellent, at times original'), for its occasional humour and for its bitter-sweet treatment of its fairy-tale subject. It is a film one regrets losing.

Between 1927 and 1929 Renoir found himself involved in a number of filmic *jeux d'esprit* among friends. Outside the mainstream film industry, in the milieu of the Parisian avant-garde, he had a role in three short films by the expatriate, Brazilian film-maker Alberto Cavalcanti and made a film of his own in atelier-like conditions. In the summer of 1927 Catherine Hessling starred in the title role of Cavalcanti's *La*

OPPOSITE TOP
Still from 'La Fille de l'eau' (1925)
Virginie sits in the window of her attic room at the Raynal farm where she gazes into her past and wonders about her future.

OPPOSITE BOTTOM LEFT
Still from 'La Fille de l'eau' (1925)
Georges pleads his love to Virginie in the garden of the Raynal farm. This sort of innocence is rare in Renoir's later work.

OPPOSITE BOTTOM RIGHT
Still from 'La Fille de l'eau' (1925)
Georges and Virginie are in the farmhouse kitchen. He is entrusting her with some purchases, but she will be accosted and robbed by Uncle Jeff.

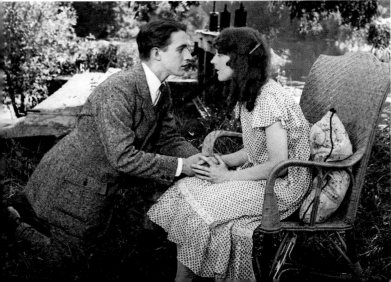

ABOVE
Still from 'Nana' (1926)
Nana (Catherine Hessling) in her dressing room
early in the film as she entertains Count Muffat
for the first time. Her doll-like appearance is
evident from the pose and makeup.

OPPOSITE
On the set of 'Nana' (1926)
Jean Bachelet stands on an elevated platform to
film the opening sequence on the stage set of
'The Blonde Venus'. Nana and Bordenave
(Pierre Lestringuez) can be seen at the ladder.

P'tite Lilie and Renoir was given a secondary part. Although he had little to do with its production, *La P'tite Lili* was an eventful film for Renoir, personally and professionally, since the three women with whom his life and career would be most entwined were all present. This shoot may have been the occasion of his first meeting with Dido Freire, the woman who would become his second wife. She probably came to her small part in the film because, like Cavalcanti, she too was an expatriate Brazilian, a daughter of the consul general in Liverpool. Furthermore, the editor on this film was Marguerite Houllé, whom he also met for the first time. She would be Renoir's companion throughout the 1930s following his separation from Catherine in 1931. In the summer of 1929 Renoir produced, co-scripted and appeared as the wolf in Cavalcanti's tongue-in-cheek adaptation of Little Red Riding Hood, *Le Petit Chaperon Rouge*. This was followed by a part in a spoof of movie trailers entitled *Vous verrez la semaine prochaine*. All of these efforts were vehicles for Catherine Hessling.

La Petite marchande d'allumettes (*The Little Match Girl*), made in the atelier of the Théâtre Vieux-Colombier Theatre in the fall of 1927, was also a Catherine Hessling vehicle and also drew upon some of the personnel who moved in the Cavalcanti circle. Basically, Renoir and Jean Tedesco used ingenuity and second-hand materials to create their own film studio. They rigged it up to produce the desired special effects for this adaptation of the Hans Christian Andersen story. Especially remarkable was their successful solution of the lighting required to expose panchromatic film indoors.

From Andersen's story, Renoir kept the New Year's Eve setting and the idea of the visions kindled by Karen's store of matches. The film contrasts the cold and isolation of the poor match seller's plight with the bright spectacle of the lives of the rich and well-fed. In her poverty Karen is doomed to be forever on the outside looking in at a world of luxury and privilege. Renoir pushed his special effects to the limit in animating the toys Karen brings to life in the hallucinations brought on when she collapses in the snow from cold and hunger. Like Alice passing through the looking-glass, Karen enters a magic world in which she and the toys are to the same scale. When the young officer of the wooden soldiers tries to spirit Karen away on horseback above the clouds, they are pursued by the figure of Death, who of course vanquishes them both. The soldier falls through the sky (like Virginie in *La Fille de l'eau*), while Karen is laid on her grave and a strand of her hair metamorphoses to a bouquet of flowers. The moral of the film may be the inescapability of death, but what one remembers is the charm of Karen's wish-fulfilling dream world in the toy shop.

When *The Little Match Girl* was first shown to a unanimously favourable press in the summer of 1928, it ran more than twenty minutes longer than the version that remains today. Unfortunately, in nervous reaction to a lawsuit for plagiarism that was eventually dismissed as utterly groundless, Renoir cut almost the whole first act of his film and part of his ending. This missing footage was designed to detail Karen's personal and social situation in relation to the upper-class world of Axel, the young man who becomes the officer in Karen's dream. However, when all is said and done, the social interest of the film as we have it now is highly conventional.

Renoir next landed a commercial project. *Tire-au-flanc* (1928) was a well-known farce in the tradition of military vaudeville (a peculiarly French genre) which had been produced many times on the stage. It brought Renoir together with Michel Simon for the first time and allowed both of them to push the limits of slapstick

ABOVE
Publicity photo for 'Nana' (1926)
An unhappy looking Nana is framed by candelabra in her bedroom. The setting and framing suggest her coldness and decadence.

OPPOSITE
Still from 'Nana' (1926)
Nana, in arrogant profile, is portrayed at the height of her sexual attraction and of her power over men.

comedy. ('Tirer au flanc' is to be a scrimshanker.) Joseph (Simon) is a servant in the household of a scatter-brained poet, Jean d'Ombelles, played by Georges Pomiès. Joseph is in love with the maid, Georgette, and Jean with his cousin, Solange. Both are called up for military service and are assigned to the same company barracks under Lt. Daumel. Barracks life is a misery for Jean, who proves to be more inept than every uniformly inept soldier. The worst of it is the bullying he must suffer at the hands of the hyper-masculine Muflot. Furthermore, Solange turns out to be more attracted to Lt. Daumel than to Jean, so Georgette pushes him in the direction of Solange's younger sister, Lily. After considerable complications of the plot, Jean exacts his revenge on Muflot (and, incidentally, on the military establishment and on polite society) at a grand fête given by the Colonel. The film ends with the formation of three happy couples: Jean and Lily, Joseph and Georgette, and Lt. Daumel and Solange.

Tire-au-flanc is a very enjoyable film, expertly performed and extremely funny. It is the most aesthetically accomplished of Renoir's silent films. Both the actors and the camera execute choreographies of movement unlike anything seen in Renoir's work to this point. In the opening sequence, the camera twice dollies backward and forward to punctuate changes in scene. It also swish pans a number of times both right and left as though to mimic (and exaggerate) the frantic movements of the characters. Georges Pomiès was a professional dancer and his suppleness of body is integral to his performance, whether he is the absent-minded civilian poet or the prat-falling enlisted man. In his tussles in the barracks scenes with Muflot, the bully, his bodily ingenuity as he trips, slips, sprawls and hurls about the room is extraordinary.

After laying out the basic narrative premise that sends Jean and Georges into army life, the film proceeds by way of a number of comic tableaux. There is an inoculation scene in which the brave recruits are terrified at getting their shots, and another at the military barber's in which they are shorn of hair and lice. But the best of these set-pieces involves the company on manoeuvres. In the funniest, the troop dons gas masks and stumbles about the countryside entirely blinded by their grotesque head-pieces. They end up rolling down a hill in full gear, where they tumble into a ring of schoolchildren being led on an outing (by Catherine Hessling). The collision emphasizes the basic infantilism of the soldiers. Another effective tableau is a drill with fixed bayonets in which Jean suddenly loses his timidity and becomes possessed. He thrusts at everything in sight, including fellow soldiers and the nearby officers of the regiment. Violence is exposed as random, hyper-virile and self-destructive. All of these high jinks, in the field or in the barracks, are comic and therefore childish, which ultimately has the effect of de-masculinizing both individual soldiers and the military establishment altogether. The military vaudeville is a genre of film in which men are not in control of themselves, their world or the narrative. In terms of the machinery of the plot here, it is actually women (and Georgette in particular), not men, who orchestrate its eventual outcome. The climax is a theatrical performance during a fête (Jean as a faun, Joseph as a nymph) whose staging goes awry (fireworks, an audience drenched) with potentially dire consequences for Jean until the intervention of Georgette. In a chronotope common to Renoir's work, the film closes with an epilogue of the newly-formed couples at dinner, thus returning us to the beginning and its opening meal. The spirit of conviviality and communal well-being around good food and drink bridges all differences.

ABOVE
Still from 'Nana' (1926)
The luxury of Nana's station is conveyed by this shot of her bath attended by her maid Zoë (Valeska Gert). This shot does not appear in most prints of the film.

OPPOSITE
Publicity photo for 'Nana' (1926)
This stunning portrait of Catherine Hessling does not appear in the film as we have it, but may belong to a lost scene or to an alternative version of the film.

ABOVE
On the set of 'Nana' (1926)
Nana's bed of concupiscence is large enough for four people: Pierre Lestringuez, Catherine Hessling, Werner Krauss and Jean Renoir.

OPPOSITE
On the set of 'Nana' (1926)
Renoir, in dark glasses, stands behind the camera as the crew films Muffat's (Werner Krauss') final ascent up the grand staircase of the Paris townhouse set to visit the dying Nana.

ABOVE
Still from 'Charleston' (1927)
A broken Eiffel Tower as a national symbol suggests the impotence of France's claim to represent European culture in the face of its colonialist history.

TOP
Still from 'Charleston' (1927)
A medium shot of Catherine Hessling doing the Charleston, her 'danse sauvage', as a dance of courtship for the benefit of Johnny Hudgins.

LEFT
Still from 'Charleston' (1927)
This is the street set for the film with Catherine Hessling as the savage, European dancer and Johnny Hudgins as the civilized, African explorer in a post-apocalyptic Paris.

ABOVE
Still from 'Marquitta' (1927)
Marquitta (Marie-Louise Iribe) listens to the protestations of Prince Vlasco (Jean Angelo) in one of the few remaining stills from this lost film.

RIGHT
Still from 'Marquitta' (1927)
This spectacular view from the corniche high above the Mediterranean shows Prince Vlasco's abortive suicide attempt near the film's end.

**Still from 'La Petite Marchande d'allumettes'
(1928)**
Karen (Catherine Hessling) is discovered dead
from cold and hunger in the snow at the
conclusion of the film.

Both of Renoir's last two silent films were produced by the Société des films historiques, a company which specialised in historical and exotic pictures. *Le Tournoi* (The Tournament, 1928), is exotic by virtue of its period setting and *Le Bled* (1929) by virtue of its Algerian locations. Both, for Renoir, were thoroughly commercial projects made with many of the same cast and crew.

Le Tournoi was commissioned for the 2000th anniversary of the founding of the city of Carcassonne. The exteriors were shot on and around the city's impressive medieval fortifications and the interiors on lavish sets at the Saint Maurice Studios. The narrative is an historical melodrama set during the 16th century, the period of Catherine de' Medici's influence at the French court of Charles IX. To keep religious peace, Catherine gives the hand of the Catholic Isabelle Ginori to the Protestant villain, François de Baynes. De Baynes wounds Isabelle's true lover, Henri de Rogier, but is killed when his murder of Isabelle's brother is made public. All ends happily (although Catholics and Protestants will go on killing one another for a long time yet). Much of the effect of *Le Tournoi* depends on its pageantry, the pomp and ceremony of court, the horsemanship during the film's tournament set-piece, duels and sword play and, of course, splendid period costumes and props. In other words, it offers itself up as a kind of cinematic tourism. The film is too long and too tedious to warrant sustained interest. The commercial circumstances of production afforded little opportunity for innovation, although for one scene Renoir mounted the camera on a makeshift contraption which allowed it to dolly the length of a banquet table in the great hall. For years the complete film was thought to be lost, until a print showed up in the 1970s. Nevertheless, it is seldom seen.

Le Bled is the more interesting and undervalued film, although it, too, has been seldom seen. Interestingly, Renoir does not mention the film in his autobiography. After *Tire-au-flanc*, however, it may be the most satisfying of Renoir's silent films. *Le Bled* was an expensive project made to commemorate the 100th anniversary of the French possession of Algeria in 1830. Part of the point, therefore, was to put Algeria on display: the exoticism of its desert locales; a gazelle hunt and a demonstration of falconry; the manners and customs of its native inhabitants. But above all the aim was to showcase the fecundity of the land farmed by its *pieds-noirs*. An eyewitness

LEFT
Still from 'La Petite Marchande d'allumettes' (1928)
As she lights matches for warmth, a kaleidoscope of light expands to reveal the hallucinatory visions brought on by Karen's fatigue and hunger.

ABOVE
Still from 'La Petite Marchande d'allumettes' (1928)
The figure of Death (Manuel Raaby) places Karen's body on her grave. The cross will catch a strand of her hair and blossom into a bouquet of flowers.

ABOVE
On the set of 'La Petite Marchande d'allumettes' (1928)
Jean Storm and Catherine Hessling are filmed on horseback by a handheld camera for the complicated montage sequence in which they are pursued through the sky by the figure of Death.

OPPOSITE TOP
On the set of 'La Petite Marchande d'allumettes' (1928)
On the sand dunes at Marly, the crew bury the camera in a bucket under a pole, so that Death's jumping horse can be filmed from below.

OPPOSITE BOTTOM
On the set of 'La Petite Marchande d'allumettes' (1928)
Renoir observes Manuel Raaby (as the figure of Death) flash past during the filming of the pursuit through the sky against the backdrop of the sand dunes.

account of the filming from 1929 makes it clear that the film was intentionally shot in locations that would highlight the touristic and commercial attractions of Algeria, with scenes set in Algiers, at the port of Sidi Ferruch, at Staouéli and on the plain of Mitidja in the south.[11] Military conquest has been transmogrified into willing pacification of a people and their land. One of the film's major set-pieces conveys this by way of an historical flashback which has the invading French forces of 1830 dissolve into a parade of tractors as they march across the landscape.

Around this colonialist political vision is woven a colonialist melodrama about competing claims to an inheritance between Claudie and her cousins, Diane and Manuel, and a sorry intrigue on the part of the latter. There is also a love affair between Claudie and Pierre, nephew of a wealthy landowner, an extraordinary gazelle hunt (the film's second major set-piece), a pursuit in the desert, the blinding of Manuel's camel by trained falcons, and the reunion of the lovers (who both come into enormous properties and presumably secure the future of Algeria as French).

ABOVE
Still from 'Tire-au-flanc' (1928)
On military manoeuvres, Joseph (Michel Simon) does his best to look and act ferociously while attempting to bayonet a dummy.

OPPOSITE
Still from 'Tire-au-flanc' (1928)
Joseph acts the part of an unlikely nymph in the makeshift theatricals which conclude the film.

Still from 'Le Tournoi' (1928)
This duel involving the professional swordsman Aldo Nadi as François de Baynes was filmed at the base of one of the towering walls around the old city of Carcassonne.

The critic André Bazin dismissed *Le Bled* as a 'technical absurdity' because he thought its shallow depth of field contrary to Renoir's consistent use of deep focus in later work.[12] If, by design, there is little depth of field here, there is nevertheless a great deal of camera movement as Renoir pans and tracks liberally to take in the landscape or to follow figure movement. One outstanding example is the extended track down the table of diners when Pierre appears for supper at his uncle's farm for the first time. The track is followed by a rapid tilt up his body to catch his startled reaction to the assembled company. Notwithstanding its propagandistic subject-matter, the experience of *Le Bled* did inspire Renoir with the idea of returning to Algeria to shoot there again at the end of the 1930s, after the completion of *La Règle du jeu*. Alas, this was an idea never to be realized. *Le Bled* was Renoir's first collaboration with Jacques Becker, who has a small part as a workman. Becker was Renoir's assistant for many years, until becoming a major director in his own right during the Second World War.

As the silent period came to a close, Renoir had served his apprenticeship well. He had acquired a technical facility and experimented with many of the stylistic

Still from 'Le Tournoi' (1928)
François de Baynes, the traitor, lies dying on the ground where the film's showpiece tournament has just taken place.

Still from 'Le Tournoi' (1928)
The queen confronts the captain of the watch and a guard. The producers spent a lot of money on the spectacle, with careful attention to costumes, sets and armaments.

ABOVE
Still from 'Le Bled' (1929)
Claudie (Jackie Monnier) is appalled at the cruelty of the gazelle hunt. This sequence anticipates the hunt in 'The Rules of the Game' ten years hence.

RIGHT
Still from 'Le Bled' (1929)
Native and French forces confront one another amidst ancient ruins that tell of the long history of European conquest in North Africa.

practices that would inform his later work. An example is his liberal use of camera movement, especially because it served to follow the actors and to locate them in their milieux. He had also formed professional associations and personal friendships that would carry forward into future collaborations, with Marguerite Houllé, Dido Freire, Pierre Braunberger (the producer), Jacques Becker, Jean Bachelet (the cameraman), the actors Max Dalban, Michel Simon and others. It was time to move forward and open new conversations.

ABOVE
Still from 'Le Bled' (1929)
In the film's climactic pursuit, Manuel Duvernet (Manuel Raaby), the villain, is stopped in his tracks when his camel is blinded by trained falcons.

TOP LEFT
Still from 'Le Bled' (1929)
A picturesque Algeria was part of the film's selling point, which partly explains this image of camels and tribesmen marshalled in the desert.

LEFT
Still from 'Le Bled' (1929)
Conquering French troops arrive in Algeria in 1830. They dissolve into a fleet of tractors. Ahead of them walk the farmer Christian Hoffer (Alexandre Arquillère) and his nephew, Pierre (Enrique Rivero).

A Social and Political Cinema 1930–1939

The film historian Georges Sadoul thought that Renoir's films of the 1930s comprised 'a social inventory of our time.'[13] This is certainly the period of Renoir's most prolific output, with fifteen films in ten years. It is also the period of his most public social and political activism, when he wrote widely for various papers and magazines on the French left. Taken together, his films of this period offer something like a composite picture of French society. Their subject matter includes a petit-bourgeois cashier's fall into the Paris underworld; a sub-proletarian tramp's encounter with the hypocrisies of the middle-class; Emma Bovary's sorry dreams of escape from her stifling provincial milieu; a crime of passion among immigrant labourers; the formation of a cooperative by skilled workers; an analysis of the gap between rich and poor; class sympathies and class divisions among prisoners of war; the march on Paris of militant revolutionaries; and, to close out the decade, a portrait of the moral corruption of France's *haute bourgeoisie* on the eve of war. Renoir may not have set out deliberately to chronicle the structures of French society, but by the end of the decade he was widely recognized as a film-maker with a social conscience who had committed himself to change. This commitment was especially evident after 1935, when the intellectual and cultural left pinned their hopes for the transformation of society on the coalition of left-wing parties known as the Popular Front (much to the chagrin of the French right).

Although film historians do not think of Renoir as a genre film-maker, it is nevertheless true that in addition to his social concerns during the 1930s he worked through most of the generic possibilities of the period. He made a farce, a boulevard comedy, a *film policier*, literary adaptations, a Neorealist film (*avant la lettre*), a 'Slav film', an experimental documentary, a period film, a war film, an historical epic, an example of poetic realism, and a comedy of manners. Against the measure of most efforts in these genres at the time, Renoir's achievement is exemplary. Notwithstanding commercial realities, what Renoir accomplishes at the limits of generic constraint puts him well beyond the workmanlike, jack-of-all-trades approach of a Julien Duvivier or a Pierre Colombier, equally prolific film-makers of the day who also worked in most genres.

During the silent period, Renoir pushed against the boundaries of what cinema could do with the means available to it. The arrival of sound was no exception to his embrace of the new. Some colleagues (famously, René Clair) deplored the advent of

ABOVE
Still from 'On purge bébé' (1931)
M. Chouilloux (Michel Simon) believes himself to have been cuckolded and in his anxiety drinks the purgative intended for little Toto.

OPPOSITE
On the set of 'On purge bébé' (1931)
With Renoir's encouragement, assistant director Claude Heymann drinks from one of the chamber pots that litter the film.

'And in 1929 a monster was born which was to stand the whole business on its head – the talkies. I welcomed it with delight, seeing at once all the use that could be made of sound. After all, the purpose of all artistic creation is the knowledge of man, and is not the human voice the best means of conveying the personality of a human being?'

Jean Renoir

ound as the death of cinema. Renoir was ready for the potential it offered to increase the range of cinematic forms, styles and subject-matters. The advent of sound (speech, music, effects and a newfound value in silence) brought to Renoir's style a realism commensurate with his social concerns and political advocacy. Acting styles, it is true, became more naturalistic with the demands of everyday speech. But the camera too in Renoir's hands became an extension of the environments and their ambient sounds in which his stories took place. The settings are no longer simply environments there to be photographed, from the outside looking in. The camera penetrates or withdraws, travels or lingers as though it were an actor in the drama as well as a witness to what unfolds before it. Nothing conveys this new relationship to setting throughout Renoir's work in this period better than those moments when the camera occasionally wanders away from the action at hand to show us something apparently off to one side, something apparently irrelevant to the story-line. Such *temps morts* in Renoir's work were the bane of producers and occasionally reviewers, who deplored the slackness of his narratives. Because of this new realism of sound and image, the spectator has a powerful sense of the immediacy of place in Renoir's work. Locations become readily identifiable and particular and their identity is integral to the pleasure and meanings of his films. In short, sound and image concretize the world; they historicize it. This makes Renoir's work of this decade an important documentary record as well as one of the greatest fictional representations in any medium, whether film, art, literature or music.

Renoir did not embark on his 1930s career without being tested. A reputation held over from the 1920s for taking risks technically, stylistically and in choice of subject-matter did not necessarily endear him to producers who expected a reasonable return on their investment. Renoir would have to prove himself with sound before he would be permitted to explore its full potential to his own ends with a large budget. The test he was set was the adaptation of a farce by Georges Feydeau called *On purge bébé*, made for Roger Richebé and Pierre Braunberger in March 1931. Renoir has often recounted his success at passing this test, inasmuch as the film was said to have taken three weeks to complete from script to screen. This was a period when adaptations dominated French production because of the need for ready dialogue during the rapid adjustment to sound. According to Renoir, a major factor contributing to this success was the novelty of recording a flushing toilet with direct sound (albeit off-screen). This latter achievement gives some idea of the drift of the film's subject matter. M. Fallavoine would like to win the lucrative contract to supply chamber pots to the French army. To this end, he has to entertain M. Chouilloux (played by Michel Simon, in his second role with Renoir), who represents the interests of the military. Unfortunately, the Fallavoine model chamber pot does not prove to be unbreakable, while M. Chouilloux becomes caught up in a misunderstanding that leads him to believe that he has been cuckolded (by a character played by Fernandel). Against this plot development is the one involving the constipated seven-year-old Toto Fallavoine and Mme. Julie Fallavoine's efforts to persuade him to take a purgative. To one way of thinking, this is a film (and a play) all about a displacement of the blockage that exists in the Fallavoine marriage. At the conclusion, since Toto does not drink the purgative intended for him, and M. Chouilloux does instead, therefore none of the impediments in the marriage have been unblocked. However, if *On purge bébé* were not a film by Renoir, it would be another of those forgotten works of the early 1930s stodgily adapted from theatre. The whole of the action is confined to three or four sets and the camera is almost

OPPOSITE TOP
Still from 'La Chienne' (1931)
Maurice Legrand (Michel Simon) works on his self-portrait as his wife, Adèle (Magdeleine Berubet), nags him and compares him unfavourably with her first husband (in photo above her). This film shows Renoir's sophisticated use of multi-level space, where the characters and camera move to use and reveal space beyond the windows and doors of their intimate environment.

OPPOSITE BOTTOM LEFT
Still from 'La Chienne' (1931)
Lulu, the prostitute (Janie Marèse), whom Legrand is keeping in her own flat, sneers at his overtures.

OPPOSITE BOTTOM RIGHT
Still from 'La Chienne' (1931)
Lulu and her pimp, Dédé (Georges Flamant). Flamant said that he used to get Janie Marèse to do what he wanted by having her lie naked for hours without touching her.

ABOVE
Still from 'La Chienne' (1931)
Lulu, surrounded by art critics and dealers, masquerades as the artist 'Clara Wood' in order to sell Legrand's paintings.

RIGHT
Still from 'La Chienne' (1931)
Legrand sees one of his paintings by 'Clara Wood' in the window of a fashionable Paris gallery. He knows he has been duped.

OPPOSITE
Still from 'La Chienne' (1931)
Across the threshold from outside to inside of Lulu's apartment, we bear witness to her dead body sprawled on the bed while Legrand stands over her.

ABOVE
Still from 'La Nuit du carrefour' (1932)
A car cuts through the night in Renoir's atmospheric precursor to French and American film noir.

OPPOSITE TOP
Still from 'La Nuit du carrefour' (1932)
Inspector Maigret (Pierre Renoir) confronts Else Andersen (Winna Winfried) in her dimly lit room filled with mysterious objects and furnishings.

OPPOSITE BOTTOM
Still from 'La Nuit du carrefour' (1932)
Maigret inspects Else's tattoo, which adds an additional element to the sexual mystery that surrounds her.

entirely static. In effect, this is a play by Feydeau more than it is a film by Renoir. It is carried by the dialogue and the actors, and especially by the performance of Marguerite Pierry, who is quite wonderful as the slovenly, utterly plain-spoken, anti-bourgeois bourgeois wife and mother.

If *On purge bébé* cannot be said to have contributed much to Renoir's concern with making people's social relations intelligible to them by means of the cinema, his next film was a different story (literally and metaphorically). Because of his success with the Feydeau, he was entrusted by the same producers with the adaptation of a contemporary novel by Georges de la Fouchardière entitled *La Chienne* (remade by Fritz Lang in 1945 as *Scarlet Street*). Unlike the studio-bound *On purge bébé*, *La Chienne* (*The Bitch*, 1931), starring Michel Simon, is set in Montmartre and numerous scenes take advantage of the possibilities for location shooting.

Running downhill away from Place Emile Goudeau (location of the famous Bateau-Lavoir Studio) in Montmartre is rue Ravignan. The facade of no.1 *bis* on the right-hand side served as the exterior of the apartment in which Legrand (Michel Simon), the Sunday painter, sets up house with Lulu (Janie Marèse), the prostitute, in *La Chienne*. Legrand leads a suffocating existence as a cashier for a hosiery company and is married to a woman who berates him constantly. In order to maintain Lulu in an apartment, he steals from his company. Legrand is unaware that

Lulu and her pimp, Dédé (Georges Flamant), have been carrying on their own relationship and selling his paintings at considerable profit as the work of the fictitious "Clara Wood". In Lulu's fifth-floor bedroom, whose window looks on to the street, the timid M. Legrand murders Lulu with a paper knife for betraying him with her pimp Dédé and above all for belittling his masculinity. But as he does so, the camera cuts from the interior of the bedroom to attend to a street singer and his entourage on the pavement below. The camera then tilts back up the façade of the building, fades to black, and then approaches the open window through which we discover Legrand leaning over Lulu's dead body. The sounds of the street singer's love song form an ironic counterpoint. Legrand manages his departure while everyone is distracted by the performance on the street. Because Dédé happens to be observed at the scene of the crime, he is tried and executed for the murder. This Montmartre, conventionally, is the scene of pleasure and crime, artists and models, sex and death. For his part, Legrand falls out of society completely and becomes a tramp on the street, the role that Michel Simon will play again in Renoir's *Boudu sauvé des eaux* two films later.

The way in which Renoir handles the murder in *La Chienne*, with the camera both crossing and linking the threshold between the public and private spheres, is typical of the way in which he handles a number of such climactic murders in a

ABOVE
Still from 'Boudu sauvé des eaux' (1932)
Through the iris of M. Lestingois' telescope, we can see Boudu (Michel Simon) preparing to jump from the Pont des Arts.

TOP RIGHT
Still from 'Boudu sauvé des eaux' (1932)
Boudu and his dog have the same curly hair, one fair, one dark. The loss of his dog makes Boudu disconsolate enough to attempt suicide.

RIGHT
Still from 'Boudu sauvé des eaux' (1932)
Boudu is surly at being divested of his clothes while M. Lestingois (Charles Granval) prepares to offer him some of his cast-offs.

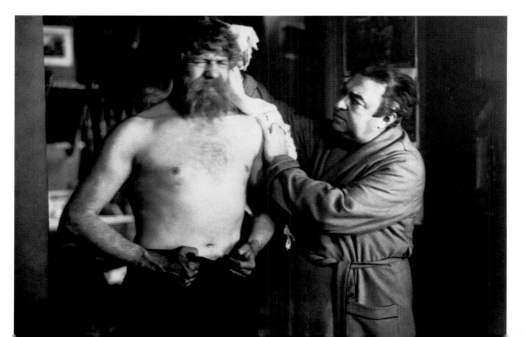

number of his 1930s films. The threshold is one of the most important chronotopes in Renoir's work during this decade. The whole of society seems implicated in what is nominally a private act. Renoir's point here, as in the other films to come, is the formative role of environment in defining who one is and what one does. As he writes in the 'Foreword' to *My Life and My Films*: 'For my part, I believe that every human creature, artist or otherwise, is largely the product of his environment. It is arrogance which leads us to believe in the supremacy of the individual... We do not exist through ourselves alone but through the environment that shaped us.'[14] So important to Renoir's work is the whole of one's environment in creating one's identity that with *La Chienne* he began the practice of working with direct sound recording. What we hear someone say, the music we overhear, or the sound effects that we hear unconsciously (famously, in *La Chienne*, a moment with water running in a gutter), are all recorded on location as closely as that is possible. When *La Chienne* was temporarily taken away from Renoir in the editing room (more troubles with producers), part of what was lost at the hands of a clumsy editor was some of his direct sound. Renoir's attention to the milieu in which his action takes place is also evident from the argot which the pimp, Dédé, and Lulu, the prostitute speak. He also does something with his camera that he will do again in other films, much to the chagrin of producers and, occasionally, critics. There are moments in *La Chienne* when the camera wanders away from the action at hand as though distracted by something going on which is no less interesting. A particularly memorable example in *La Chienne* occurs when we hear someone playing scales somewhere off-screen, and the camera then ignores Legrand in his own apartment to pick up a little girl seated at a piano through the window of a neighbouring apartment. She does not figure in the plot at all, but she is part of Legrand's extended milieu and her playing does remind us of the incidental detail that makes up so much of daily life.

The producers of *La Chienne* were worried that such a sordid story would have a limited exhibition and lose money. Fortunately, Léon Siritzky, the owner of a cinema chain, took matters in hand with a publicity campaign built around the film's anticipated shock value, a strategy designed to ensure audience curiosity and a good box office. The film's success may also have been helped by the fact that the Legrand-Lulu-Dédé triangle in the film was imitated in real life. Unfortunately, Janie Marèse (Lulu) was killed in an automobile accident with Georges Flamant (Dédé) at the wheel, leaving Michel Simon as disconsolate as his M. Legrand. Ironically, Renoir's commitment to Marèse as Lulu had precipitated his break-up with Catherine Hessling in 1931, which led to his relationship with Marguerite Houllé, his film editor, through the remainder of the 1930s.

A reel or two of Renoir's next film, *La Nuit du carrefour* (*Night at the Crossroads*, 1932), are either lost or not shot at all. One way or the other this was an oversight which does nothing for the spectator's ease of comprehension. The film is the first screen adaptation of a closely plotted Inspector Maigret detective story by Georges Simenon. However, in terms of what counts here, the loss of footage and potential plot confusion contribute greatly to the film's remarkable atmosphere: 'My aim was to convey by imagery the mystery of that starkly mysterious tale, and I meant to subordinate the plot to the atmosphere.'[15] This atmosphere is what makes *La Nuit du carrefour* very much a film of modern life. It was filmed on location in the middle of winter at an isolated crossroads in the country outside of Paris. The rain, the mud, the fog, the cold (we can see the breath of the characters), and what seems like

Still from 'Boudu sauvé des eaux' (1932)
Boudu relishes sardines and bread, but finds white wine too sharp for his rough tastes.

TOP LEFT
Still from 'Boudu sauvé des eaux' (1932)
Boudu shares a laugh with Lestingois. Three images on this page show Boudu interacting with each of the other characters. In the fourth they set him apart because of his anarchy.

TOP RIGHT
Still from 'Boudu sauvé des eaux' (1932)
Mme. Lestingois (Marcelle Hainia) is not impressed by Boudu's ungrateful manners or his disruption of her household.

BOTTOM LEFT
Still from 'Boudu sauvé des eaux' (1932)
Boudu's relationship with Anne-Marie, the maid (Séverine Lerczinska), is playful and teasing, as well as frustrating, because she is closer to him in station.

BOTTOM RIGHT
Still from 'Boudu sauvé des eaux' (1932)
The three permanent members of the household look like they are conspiring against Boudu. Having him marry the maid would be one solution.

OPPOSITE
On the set of 'Boudu sauvé des eaux' (1932)
Everybody waits for the next setup, including Michel Simon in the centre and Renoir partially hidden on the right, while the script girl makes a forceful point.

perpetual night convey a sense of space having closed in and of time as completely open. After Maigret is alerted to the murder of a diamond merchant in a car at the crossroads, the plot concerns the exposure of an organized smuggling ring run out of the local garage. None of the plot details much matters. What matters are the camera set-ups which obscure more than they reveal, because our view is blocked by interfering objects in the foreground or middle ground. A car chase along country roads at night is filmed at night, so that we see next to nothing. And nothing is what it seems in this film. Everything seems to suggest itself as a troubled symptom of something else: Danish spoken by Else and Carl; her surrealist paintings; a live tortoise with a decorated shell; shadowy figures in a ghostly landscape; a poached rabbit; the direct sound of unseen cars passing in the dark; neurotic hand movements; a tap dripping into a full glass of water, etc. All of these effects, of the setting, of the camera, of the lighting, and of the *mise en scène* convey a sense that the experience of modernity is thoroughly alienating, both psychologically and socially. *La Nuit du carrefour* is a fascinating precursor of French and American film noir and all those films set at unforgiving motels and lonely crossroads, in fog-shrouded environments or deadly night, like *The Postman Always Rings Twice* (made in French, Italian and twice in English), *Le Quai des brumes*, *The Killers*, or *The Big Sleep*. In some quarters, *La Nuit du carrefour* stands out as the best Simenon adaptation with the best Maigret ever filmed.

France was in the grip of the Depression and the city of Paris was haunted by vagrants in the summer of 1932 when Renoir adapted René Fauchois' comic drama *Boudu sauvé des eaux* (*Boudu Saved From Drowning*) about a middle-class bookseller who fishes a tramp out of the Seine. (The film was remade badly by Paul Mazursky as *Down and Out in Beverly Hills* in 1986 with Nick Nolte, and somewhat better by Gérard Jugnot as *Boudu* in 2005, with Gérard Depardieu in the title role). The antics of the film are built around the brilliant performance of Michel Simon in the role of the exuberant title character, and when Renoir recalled the film many years later he described it as 'a free exercise around an actor.'[16] To make a play first performed in 1919 topical for 1932, Renoir re-invented most of its first two acts and changed its ending so that he could move as much of its action as possible outside into the Paris of everyday life. The effect of the film is therefore more successful if the spectator can recognize the importance of its settings (none of which has changed since 1932).

We first discover Boudu, the sub-proletarian tramp, in the Bois de Boulogne, where he loses his dog and has fleeting encounters with a cross-section of the more upright and respectable, if conventional inhabitants of the city (mothers and children, a poet, a motorist or two, a gendarme, etc.). Beside himself at losing his dog, Boudu wanders into the city centre along the quays past the bouquinistes. He arrives at the Pont des Arts where he attempts suicide by throwing himself into the Seine. M. Lestingois' bookshop is located at the south end of the Pont des Arts. He makes a habit of watching the women through his telescope pass along the quay. He spies Boudu as "a perfect specimen" of a tramp and sees his jump from the bridge. There is a wonderful, extended, naturalistic sequence on the river with the boat traffic and the crowds on the bridge as Lestingois rescues Boudu. To the consternation of Mme. Lestingois and the dismay of Anne-Marie, the maid, Lestingois takes Boudu into their home and the bookshop where he feeds him, dresses him (in his cast-offs), and endeavours to tutor him in the attractions of a bourgeois lifestyle. Boudu, however, will have none of it, and is all disruptive force, an untrammelled sexual

On the set of 'Madame Bovary' (1933)
Lunch by the side of the road. As usual in these group shots, Renoir is never front and centre, but, in the spirit of egalitarianism, one among the collective.

energy, who turns the household upside down and inside out. He frustrates M. Lestingois' nightly trysts with Anne-Marie, seduces Mme. Lestingois, and inadvertently exposes the moral hypocrisy and cultural snobbery of the bourgeois life. Efforts at explaining to Boudu why one should wear a tie, polish one's shoes or use a handkerchief are met with anarchic resistance. With obvious irony, Lestingois is shown to be outraged that Boudu would spit in a first edition of Balzac's *Physiologie du mariage.* "One should only rescue one's own kind," concedes M. Lestingois. Renoir's camera draws attention to the confinement of the bookshop interiors with occasional pans and tracks and by shooting through doorways and windows. Matters are apparently resolved when Boudu wins the lottery and is to marry Anne-Marie. However, as the wedding party drifts on the Marne, Boudu overturns the boat, floats away with the current and leaves everyone else to dry out on the shore. He is "a wild animal", concludes Mme. Lestingois. Boudu is once again beyond the edge of the city, outside society. Lestingois and his household presumably take up where they left off before this encounter.

Little imagination is required to see Boudu as a projection of Lestingois' buried self, that he releases that which has been repressed in Lestingois beneath the veneer of bourgeois respectability. That is clear enough when we register Lestingois' excitement as Boudu is framed by his telescope. When he takes him in, Lestingois indulges Boudu as though he were a kindred spirit. Furthermore, Boudu arrives just as Lestingois admits euphemistically to Anne-Marie that his pipes are weary. So Boudu acts out what Lestingois dare not nor can no longer act out himself. But Lestingois is also intended to stand in for French society as a whole, which is why his bookshop is located in front of the Institut Français (French Institute), home to

the Académie française (the French Academy), and across from the Louvre, that is, at the very centre of a city which is itself at the very centre of a culture and a civilisation. What is exposed in Lestingois about the emptiness of bourgeois values is exposed for French society as whole, albeit that the film's satire is gentle rather than caustic.

Renoir's least memorable film may be *Chotard et Cie.* of 1933, a film Renoir himself could barely recall in interviews years later. Everything about the film seems unsympathetic to the direction of Renoir's interests and talent at this time. Like *On purge bébé, Chotard et Cie.* is one of the hundreds of French films made between 1930 and 1933 that are weighed down by their literary origins. In this case, its basis is a play by Roger Ferdinand, who also produced the film and did the adaptation. For his part, Renoir seems to have been burdened with executing someone else's work. After all, the three sound films he made previous to this were also from literary sources, but in those instances he was actively involved in their adaptation in ways that suited his inclinations. He was able to challenge the limitations of sound recording with inventive camera work and by opening up the set to the outdoors. *Chotard et Cie.* is studio-bound, apart from one unnecessary exterior scene, and betrays its theatrical origins with far too much talk, too many broad strokes (Charpin as Chotard, especially), and too many boxed camera set-ups at the expense of the possibilities of the *mise en scène*.

Art collides with commerce when the poet Julien Collinet marries Reine, the daughter of François Chotard, an extremely successful, if excessively frugal, retail food merchant. Julien is hopeless as a tradesman and is in danger of expulsion from the household. The philistine Chotard is converted to the benefits of poetry when

Still from 'Madame Bovary' (1933)
In her deathbed delirium, Madame Bovary clutches a crucifix. By dressing her in white, Renoir offers a hint of redemption for her trespasses.

Julien wins the Prix Goncourt. ("We're above money now." "That must be pretty high!") However, much to his own as well as everybody else's frustration, Julien cannot write another word and art reaches a compromise with commerce when he agrees that there is poetry to be found in trade, among the cabbages and artichokes. If this treatment seems like a detour from Renoir's emerging social and aesthetic concerns, there is nevertheless one truly outstanding shot in this film. That is the very first shot, a tour de force which lasts a full two minutes, and which begins on a close-up of the Chotard name on a crate, then pulls back and opens up the field of view through which it tracks, follows, hesitates and pans as M. Chotard arrives at his shop in the morning, greets his staff and undertakes the day's business. Beginning a moving camera shot like this in close-up (as he had once in *Nana*) is a signature Renoir effect that will have considerable import in later films. The last shot of the film is a much abbreviated version of the first, this time in reverse. How easily the film's stylistic flourishes are here divorced from its substance.

Bertolt Brecht is reported to have seen and applauded a version of Renoir's *Madame Bovary* (1934) that ran over three hours. Renoir first met Brecht while working on his adaptation of the Flaubert novel sometime in September 1933. They probably met through Carl Koch, Renoir's assistant on the film. Renoir was bilingual in French and German so they would have conversed easily. Brecht conveyed his impression of Renoir in *Esskultur*, a short story based on a dinner together with Renoir, Koch and other friends. That chronotope again! Renoir and Brecht would meet again in Hollywood in the 1940s, two European exiles among hundreds trying to make their way in an unforgiving industry. What became of the long version of *Madame Bovary* no one now knows. If it did exist it must have been cut at the insistence of Gaston Gallimard, the publisher. He backed the film financially so that Valentine Tessier, his mistress and an established stage actor, could star in the title role.

The full version of the film might have extended the long course of Emma Bovary's moral corruption as she tires of her well-meaning and devoted, but boorish husband (Charles), takes up with lovers (Rodolphe and Léon), and spends well beyond her means (with the draper Lheureux). More in the way of situation and motive might have been communicated, too, in the context of the constricting provincial environment near Rouen which leads to Mme. Bovary's deceptions of self and others. Nevertheless, Renoir's treatment of this most famous of heroines in the most famous of French novels is of considerable interest.

One effective and wholly cinematic means of getting across Emma's desire for a different sort of life, a life of excitement, is Renoir's liberal use of the horse-drawn carriage as a sustained motif. What is a thoroughly naturalistic conveyance in the time frame of the 1840s becomes suggestive of Emma's longing to be elsewhere, both physically and emotionally. Consequently, we have the crucial scene in which Charles ingenuously presents Emma with the carriage he has bought her so that she might have a fuller life. The purchase is announced in the drawing room and the window is then flung open to reveal the horse and carriage standing in deep space in the street outside. Without a cut or any movement of the camera, Emma and Charles exit the shot to reappear through the window on the street where they mount the carriage. The chronotope of the threshold between inside and outside provided by the window frame announces a moment of crisis in their relationship. Certainly the carriage suggests Emma's (potential) mobility, her ability to travel, potentially to escape, but in this shot it is also contained by the frame of the

OPPOSITE TOP LEFT
Still from 'Toni' (1935)
The kiss on the neck by which Toni (Charles Blavette) attempts to extract the wasp sting from Joséfa (Celia Montalvan) but instead becomes poisoned by his passion for her.

OPPOSITE TOP RIGHT
Still from 'Toni' (1935)
Toni and his wife, Marie (Jenny Hélia), exchange frozen glances as Toni's continuing infatuation with Joséfa is about to undo their marriage.

OPPOSITE BOTTOM
Still from 'Toni' (1935)
The wedding banquet for two unhappy couples, with Albert (Max Dalban) and Joséfa on the left, and Marie and Toni to the right. Uncle Sebastian (André Kovachevitch) is keeping them apart.

ABOVE
Still from 'Toni' (1935)
Toni cradles Marie after her suicide attempt in
the Etang de Berre as revenge for Toni's
obsession with Joséfa.

RIGHT
On the set of 'Toni' (1935)
The camera is filming Toni's last moments by the
railway tracks at film's end. This looks like a cold
day during a summer shooting schedule.

OPPOSITE
Still from 'Toni' (1935)
In one of the film's few close-ups, Joséfa cradles
the gun with which she is about to shoot
husband Albert for having brutalized her once
too often.

window. In brief, the way in which this moment is handled brilliantly conveys the
tension between the pull of Emma's desires and the real inescapability of her present
circumstances.

This scene is a very good example of Renoir's command in the 1930s of the
most naturalistic means in terms of camera, performance, and setting, for complex
effects. Such subtle means for highly suggestive ends become a trademark of his
style and show a confidence in the spectator's attentiveness to a richer
understanding of his work. This scene with the carriage is also the moment which
inaugurates the process of Emma's corruption and Charles' humiliation (which he
has inadvertently authored by giving her the carriage in the first place). The scene in
the drawing-room actually begins with Lheureux, whose eventual demand for
payment of accumulated debts at film's end will lead to Emma's suicide. The next
scene takes us with Emma and Charles as they go for a carriage ride. It concludes
with Emma's display of exhilaration, but also her first rejection of Charles' embrace.
From this moment her corruption deepens, as she next expresses her disgust at
Charles' table manners and his country boots, disowns him at the ball, hits her
demanding daughter, and refuses to kiss her husband. We know she is completely
undone when she callously smokes a cigarette while proclaiming love to Léon.
Other carriage scenes in the film follow from this first one and are woven into the
narrative course of Emma's undoing. For example, the invitation to the ball comes
as two carriages meet on the thoroughfare, the seduction scene with Léon takes
place in his carriage, and we have occasional shots of punctuation of an empty
roadway and a retreating camera.

Madame Bovary is a melodrama, that is to say it is concerned with the
vicissitudes of emotional life in social circumstances or, more especially, the
frustration of female desire in and by an oppressive and patriarchal society. The
film's portrait of this society is bitter and unforgiving. Both of Emma's lovers are
utterly feckless, her husband a Mama's boy and an incompetent surgeon, the priest
platitudinous, the lawyer lecherous, Lheureux grasping, and Homais, the pharmacist,

a cynic. In short, Emma's attempt to become the agent of her own destiny is blocked by a world which is as corrupt as it is corrupting. Consistent with the narrative goal of melodrama, however, Emma is redeemed for innocence, even if society is not, as she lies dressed in white on her deathbed and embraces the cross.

If Renoir fared much better with *Madame Bovary* aesthetically than he had with *Chotard et Cie.* the year before, he fared no better commercially. *Madame Bovary* was a box-office disaster.

Here is yet another in the long list of Renoir films which suffered the ignominy of cuts and interference at the hands of worried producers, distributors and exhibitors. Renoir was earning a reputation as a *cinéaste maudit.*

Renoir took his position as an outsider to the mainstream of the French film industry to heart with *Toni* (1934). He got as far away from Paris as he could, to the Martigues region in the south of France, and took his story from a local crime of passion of some years before (rather than from a published work, as he had heretofore). He also enlisted the help of Marcel Pagnol, who had already made a solid reputation out of regional film-making. The making of *Toni* was a milestone in Renoir's career because it allowed him to demonstrate his absolute command over the complete integration of story with setting. This was the accomplishment that earned *Toni* deserved recognition as a precursor of Italian Neorealism. Two other aspects of the production probably aided this recognition. One was the presence of Luchino Visconti and the second was the appeal of Italian and Spanish immigrant workers as the subjects of his story. Verisimilitude was achieved not only by the setting and by a story drawn from daily life. Renoir also cast professionals and non-professionals alike who were native to the region and who could speak and act with the appropriate authority.

Toni arrives in the south of France from Italy and finds work in a quarry. Many migrant workers from Spain and Italy have made this journey before and many will make it after Toni's story has ended. As a consequence of the Depression, there were over a million foreign workers in France in the early 1930s. "My country is wherever

ABOVE
Still from 'Le Crime de Monsieur Lange' (1936)
Lange (René Lefèvre) dresses up as his alter ego, Arizona Jim, while he gathers inspiration for a new story about his cowboy hero's exploits in the Far West.

LEFT
Still from 'Le Crime de Monsieur Lange' (1936)
The women in the courtyard laundry are shown working together to a common end. Estelle (Nadia Sibirskaïa) is in the middle ground of the shot.

'[Le Crime de Monsieur Lange] *is based on the idea that any man who has carved out a place for himself in society and is worthy of his position has the right to keep his place and to defend it against one who would take it from him, even if the thief bases his actions on legal principles.*'

André Bazin

ABOVE
Still from 'Le Crime de Monsieur Lange' (1936)
Estelle and Charles (Maurice Baquet) meet through a window which links courtyard exterior with bedroom interior. The use of the threshold for linking characters and spaces is common in Renoir's work.

RIGHT
Still from 'Le Crime de Monsieur Lange' (1936)
With Valentine (Florelle) looking on, Lange shoots Batala on behalf of the entire community. The unscrupulous capitalist has come back to reclaim his business disguised as a priest.

I can earn my bread," says an anonymous labourer in the film. Toni lives with Marie, who is French, but is in love with Joséfa, who is an immigrant from Spain. He hopes to marry Joséfa, leave the quarry, and work the farm with her uncle and guardian Sebastien. However, when Joséfa is raped by Albert, the quarry foreman, whom she must then marry, Toni has to settle for Marie. Disconsolate that Toni is still infatuated with Joséfa, Marie attempts suicide by throwing herself into the Etang de Berre. Matters completely unravel when Marie banishes love-sick Toni from her house and Joséfa shoots Albert for abusing her. Toni helps Joséfa wheel Albert's body away into the woods, but is caught planting a gun on the corpse. He tries to escape capture but is shot at the end of the railway trestle (the Caronte Bridge) which had carried him to the south of France at the film's beginning. Another train comes carrying another group of hopeful immigrants at film's end.

Toni is a transnational story whose characters are French, Italian, Spanish and Corsican. Its narrative and situation call into question the meaning of traditional concepts like home, belonging, place, community and identity. But the concept that is most obviously in question is that of the nation. The allegiances that unite or divide the characters in *Toni* are not so much national as determined by language, food, music, dress or custom and may take root anywhere. Because this is not the metropolis, not Paris, and little subject to influence from the capital, the south of France is the ideal environment in which to challenge essential or fixed categories of identity. It is not incidental that more of *Toni* takes place in the outdoors with direct sound than any other Renoir film of the 1930s except *Partie de campagne*. *Toni* articulates a general theme that Renoir's work will develop through the remainder of the 1930s. A society is always under pressure from its own limitations, from kinds of relations and senses of self and possibilities of difference that it has ignored or repressed or failed to develop. How it handles that pressure, artistically and socially, is therefore extremely important.

The end of *Toni* was the beginning of Renoir's committed association with the causes of the French left from the mid-1930s on. Sometime in February or March of 1934 he apparently made a brief visit to the Soviet Union, which no doubt hardened his resolve to play a part in the transformation of French society. Some of the economic and political conditions that led people like Renoir to take up strongly fortified ideological positions were the prolonged effects of the Depression, the severely unequal distribution of wealth, appalling conditions for French workers (60-hour work weeks, no vacation time), the emboldened anti-Semitism and xenophobia of the French right, and concerns about the rise and spread of Fascism in Europe. In the interest of his convictions, therefore, Renoir allied himself with various left-wing, largely Parti Communiste Français (French Communist Party), social and cultural organisations. He appeared at political functions, signed petitions and wrote for like-minded newspapers and magazines. This included a stint as a regular columnist for the paper *Ce Soir* between March 1937 and November 1938. He also made films which he intended as an intervention within unfolding current events.

The first filmic example of Renoir's explicit devotion to social change was *Le Crime de Monsieur Lange* (*The Crime of Mr. Lange*, 1936). Batala, the unscrupulous, womanising owner of a small publishing firm, exploits his workers and dupes his creditors until the point comes at which he is forced to flee the city. When the report of a train wreck apparently announces Batala's death, the workers set up a co-operative and the dreamy Monsieur Lange writes the fantastic adventure stories they print for publication. Lange's stories are set in the American Far West and are

Still from 'Le Crime de Monsieur Lange' (1936)
Valentine and Lange stand on a beach at the frontier with Belgium and wave goodbye as they head into exile. Lange has been exonerated by the frontier 'jury' for the murder of Batala.

built around the exploits of 'Arizona Jim'. He single-handedly battles evildoers who would deny the rights of women, "Negroes" and workers. Despite his timidity, Lange has fallen into a relationship with Valentine, who runs a laundry in the same courtyard as the publishing outfit. All seems to be well in love and society. Unfortunately, Batala has survived the train crash, assumed the disguise of a priest, and shows up to reclaim his former business on the very night the co-op is celebrating its good fortune. Lange shoots and kills Batala in a brilliant scene that comprises nearly a 360-degree pan which includes the entire courtyard and its community. By implication, the responsibility for Batala's death falls to everyone (both inside and outside the film). This is a good example of a variation on the chronotope of the threshold. Presumably, with its capitalist boss dead, the co-operative can continue to flourish. Lange does not have to pay for his crime, because Valentine is able to convince a 'jury' at a frontier inn to permit them to escape across the border into Belgium without alerting the police.

The film's plot is like one of those true crime stories that the co-op prints in the publishing house, only this time it serves an explicitly political and locally applicable purpose. The people have triumphed over Capital and its ally the Church right here in France, not just in far off Arizona. The film lightens what might seem like a one-dimensional political 'message' by its humour. *Le Crime de Monsieur Lange* is something like a surrealist political cartoon, with its string of comically incongruous dialogues and situations. Jacques Prévert's contribution to the screenplay and the anarchic October Group's contribution to the performances were no doubt important factors in this regard. The film is also very effective at creating a powerful sense of community amongst the inhabitants of its principal courtyard setting. In this respect the versatility of Renoir's camera in deepening space by shooting through doors and windows and moving to encompass overlapping action is remarkable.

La Vie est à nous (*Life is Ours*, 1936) was a direct commission from the Parti Communiste Français. It had no theatrical release (it was censored), but was shown instead at political meetings and Party functions. It was commissioned to promote the Party's cause in the Popular Front alliance with the Socialists and with the Radical Democrats (not actually very radical) in anticipation of the upcoming French national elections in June. The film did continue to circulate after the elections and even had an American release in 1937. *La Vie est à nous* is an enduring achievement because of its experimental character as part radical documentary, part polemical fiction. This is a film much influenced by the political theatre and agit-prop cinema of Bertolt Brecht (for example, his *Kuhle Wampe* of 1932). The theme of *La Vie est à nous* is "Work, Liberty, Peace", in response to the lasting effects of the Depression in France and the threat of war with the rise of fascism in Germany and Italy.

A schoolteacher explains to his students that France is a productive and wealthy country. After school, in the streets of a rundown suburb, his impoverished, working-class students wonder at the unequal distribution of such wealth. We are told about the "200 families" who exploit their workers even as they dissipate fortunes in gambling. Newsreel footage of the right-wing street riots of 6 February 1934 is countered by the solidarity of workers who occupy the streets in a general strike in the following days. The warmongering of Hitler and Mussolini is exposed through some gruesome footage. Their French sympathizers are mocked. The Parti Communiste Français offers the way out. Marcel Cachin, the editor of *L'Humanité*, the Party newspaper, is shown in his office reading three letters from subscribers, each of which introduces a fictional episode to illustrate the Party's support for the disadvantaged.

The first episode concerns working conditions in a factory and the successful efforts of organised workers to save the job of an older employee. In the second episode, an auction of a farm family's goods and animals is sabotaged by a sympathetic band of men who intimidate prospective bidders. They manage to buy back the family's property for a pittance. Renoir probably directed the third episode himself. It has certain hallmarks of his style in the camera set-ups and camera movements. A young engineer leaves his girlfriend out of necessity and tries unsuccessfully to find work. Hungry and on the street, he is picked up by a couple of Communists and taken to a Party gathering where he is fed and given something to do. *La Vie est à nous* ends with the casts of all three episodes gathered to listen to a succession of political speeches, followed by a public march in which they joyfully sing the 'Internationale'. The film achieves much of its effect through a certain slippage between the status accorded each of the documentary and fictional modes, so that the line between them is blurred.

'The separation of mankind into fascists and communists is quite meaningless. Fascism, like communism, believes in progress... But in the last resort one has to take up one's own stand. If I were forced to do so, with my back to the wall, I would opt for communism because it seems to me that those who believe in it have a truer conception of human dignity.'

Jean Renoir

Still from 'La Vie est à nous' (1936)
In solidarity the characters from all three of the film's sketches mingle with other workers and march toward the camera singing the 'Internationale' at the film's end.

ABOVE
Still from 'Une Partie de campagne' (1936)
Henriette (Sylvia Bataille) and Henri (Georges Darnoux) in the boat on the river that will take them to the scene of her seduction in the woods.

TOP RIGHT
Still from 'Une Partie de campagne' (1936)
In this shot, Henriette finds pleasure in the pure innocence of the swing, joyful at the release she experiences in the country.

RIGHT
Still from 'Une Partie de campagne' (1936)
Rodolphe (Jacques Brunius) seduces Mme. Dufour (Jeanne Marken) by acting the part of a satyr as he circles around her. The satyr is a recurring motif in Renoir's films.

Une Partie de campagne (*A Day in the Country*, 1936) is a fragmentary masterpiece, like Coleridge's *Kubla Khan* or Dickens' *The Mystery of Edwin Drood*. Inclement weather during the summer of 1936, which Renoir did his best to incorporate into his story, forced him to leave the film uncompleted while he left for his next engagement. Two title cards substitute for the scenes which were never shot. However, the spectator senses no lacunae in a film which seems perfectly self-contained. *Partie de campagne* is set on the Loing and its banks south of Paris in 1880, during the period of the Maupassant story from which it is adapted. The film is a 40-minute emotional tone poem, rather than a driven narrative. It captures brilliantly the vulnerability of a young woman's loss of innocence and first love. Henriette and her family, like so many Parisians, take a day in the country and have a picnic on the grass by the river's edge. Here, these city folks are out of their element and the film spares nothing in its satire of Henriette's bumbling father and her intended fiancé. For her part, Henriette experiences an unusual sympathy with nature's abundance and remarks particularly on the fragility of the tiny lives beneath her feet. Renoir himself plays the innkeeper who caters to the Dufour family as well as to Rodolphe and Henri, the local swells who will seduce the mother and daughter, respectively. The attraction of the suitors to their prey is caught by Mme. Dufour's tizziness in the sunshine and country air and by Henriette's liberating turn on a swing whose movement the camera follows with an imitative back-and-forth

motion. The country men and their city women pair off and take to the river in skiffs. The tenderness of Henriette's feelings is caught by the boat's sensuous glide on the river's surface, the overhanging banks of trees and long grasses, the song of a nightingale, and finally by a change in the weather which brings rain and disappointment. Nature is in complete sympathy with the flux of Henriette's feelings. One single shot, one of the greatest in all of Renoir's work, condenses the whole of the film's sweet melancholy. As Henriette gives into Henri's seduction, she turns her head, and her eye looks pleadingly into the eye of the camera and we know as she knows that the moment of innocence has passed. Years later, she returns to this same spot with her still clownish husband. She meets Henri by chance once again, but leaves with a heart-wrenching look that says her life is a ruin because of this memory of first love and its loss.

Partie de campagne is a good example of another of those films in Renoir's career in which he was able to experience 'the ecstasy of intimacy'. In addition to the conviviality of old friends and colleagues like Pierre Lestringuez in the part of a passing curé, there were walk-ons by new ones like Georges Bataille (now separated from Sylvia) and Henri Cartier-Bresson. There was also the presence of family with his son Alain in the part of the boy fishing on the bridge and his companion Marguerite in the role of the country waitress. Because Renoir was forced to leave *Partie de campagne* uncompleted, the film was withheld from distribution in 1936 in the expectation that he or another director might return to fill in what was missing. This was not to be, so the film was finally released to surprised audiences in 1946.

The next project which beckoned Renoir in the fall of 1936 was an adaptation of Maxim Gorki's play *Les Bas-Fonds* (*The Lower Depths*) for Albatros films. This was a production company founded by the Russian émigré community in Paris between the wars. In consequence of its source, the film's characters are Russian but its setting contemporary and Parisian. This discordance between characters and setting was no doubt intended to encourage the spectator to consider the lesson to be taken from the transposition of the Russian will to collective social action to French circumstances.

Louis Jouvet and Jean Gabin were the two greatest actors of their generation, on the stage and in the cinema respectively, and are a delight to watch playing off each other in *The Lower Depths*. Jouvet's presence as the impecunious Baron is gestural, physically prominent, right from the film's opening shot when he adopts a pose as the camera circles around him while he is being dismissed from his government position for defrauding the state. Gabin's petty thief, Pépel, is all understatement, subdued in speech and movement, until he is pushed to one of those sudden outbursts of rage which became his trademark in so many films. When Pépel is surprised attempting to rob the Baron, who no longer has anything to steal, their common plight leads them to the same flophouse with its mad, its diseased and its socially marginalized (an actor, a prostitute, an accordionist, a dispossessed shoemaker, etc.).

The Baron accepts his fate and in a remarkable river bank scene set in a working-class, industrial wasteland, while a snail crawls across his hand, he reflects on the vicissitudes of his life to Pépel as so many changes of costume. Pépel, on the other hand, finds life in the flophouse intolerable and its owner Kostylev exploitative. In a burst of anger, he kills Kostylev, surrounded by the inhabitants of this microcosm of a larger France. Like the murder of Batala in *Le Crime de Monsieur Lange*, the act is

77

Still from 'Les Bas-fonds' (1936)
The Baron and the prostitute (Jany Holt) react to the suicide of the alcoholic Actor (Robert Le Vigan). Note how all the elements of the shot pull downward.

ABOVE
Still from 'La Grande Illusion' (1937)
Boeldieu (Pierre Fresnay) and Rauffenstein
(Erich von Stroheim), the film's upper-class
career officers, converse at leisure in the fortress
prison with Rauffenstein's geranium on the
window ledge between them.

RIGHT
Still from 'La Grande Illusion' (1937)
The French prisoners of war chat while they
prepare the costumes for the camp theatricals.
The window behind them is another of those
thresholds that links an interior and an exterior
space.

ABOVE
Still from 'La Grande Illusion' (1937)
At the prison camp theatricals, Cartier, the actor (Julien Carette), leads a song and dance number backed by a bevy of cross-dressing soldiers.

LEFT
Still from 'La Grande Illusion' (1937)
There is a tender moment in the film when our main characters gather around a soldier dressed up as a woman and we imagine each of them dreaming of civilian life. Dressing-up is a recurring motif in Renoir's films.

PAGES 82/83
Still from 'La Grande Illusion' (1937)
Here is another of those crowd scenes so familiar in Renoir's work. This time it is the community of soldiers gathered to watch the prison theatricals.

ABOVE
Still from 'La Grande Illusion' (1937)
The 15th-century fortress of Haut-Koenigsburg in Alsace served as the setting for the last prison camp in the film. Rauffenstein is giving everyone a guided tour.

RIGHT
On the set of 'La Grande Illusion' (1937)
Bundled up against the bitter cold on a location scout at Haut-Koenigsburg during the winter of 1937, Renoir and his colleagues (including Jacques Becker, left, and Claude Renoir, right) discuss camera set-ups.

not only a matter of individual revenge but also a collective uprising against injustice. Nevertheless, by film's end nothing has fundamentally changed to relieve the despair of the denizens of the lower depths. The Actor, for example, has hanged himself, perhaps at the Baron's unwitting suggestion. After a term in jail, Pépel flees this world with Kostylev's daughter, Natacha. The last shot of the film, with Pépel and Natacha receding into the distance from a retreating camera, is a deliberate homage to Chaplin's *Modern Times*, which Renoir had reviewed earlier in 1936. *The Lower Depths* received the praise of the French left, earned the Prix Louis Delluc as the best French film of the year, and was ranked second among foreign releases for 1937 by the U.S. National Board of Review.

La Grande Illusion (*Grand Illusion*, 1937) is a love story, albeit that the film is set in successive prison camps and on a mountain farm during the First World War. In truth, *Grand Illusion* is a number of love stories, of man or men for a woman, of man and men for one another. There is no Renoir film in which the bond between certain characters or groups of characters is so powerful or so convincing. The film makes the case that the real barriers that divide people and lead to enmity or war are vertical frontiers like national or class differences. These are differences that arise from ideologies that segregate people between countries, or from one another within their own country. On the other hand, there is everything in common between people who are separated horizontally. These are people of the same class who share the same interests (Boeldieu and Rauffenstein, in the film) or occupation

ABOVE
Still from 'La Grande Illusion' (1937)
Maréchal (Jean Gabin) has been thrown into solitary confinement for disrupting the theatricals. His isolation is poignant, because one of the guards has given him a harmonica to help pass the time.

PAGE 86
Still from 'La Grande Illusion' (1937)
To enable fellow officers Maréchal and Rosenthal to escape the fortress, Boeldieu creates a diversion high up on the scaffolding inside the prison walls.

PAGE 87
Still from 'La Grande Illusion' (1937)
Rauffenstein takes careful aim as he prepares to shoot Boeldieu, his fellow officer. His shot wounds Boeldieu and does not kill him outright.

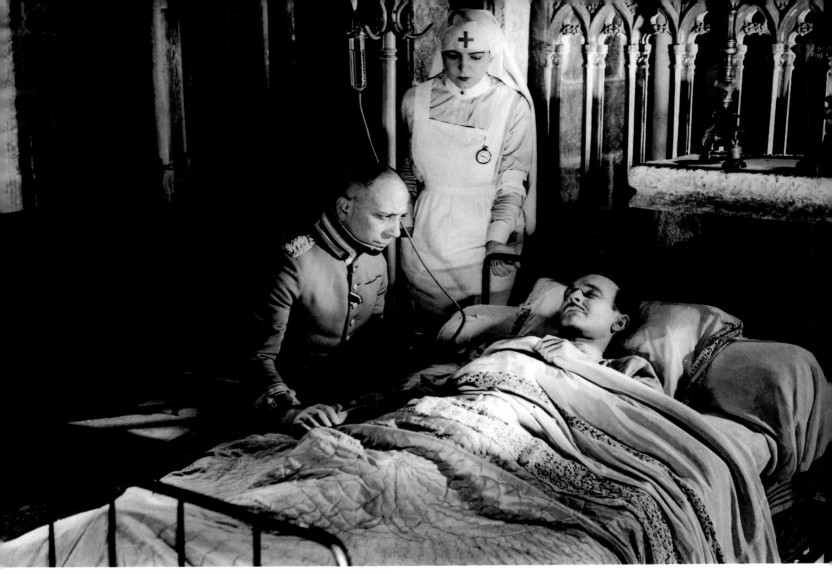

ABOVE
Still from 'La Grande Illusion' (1937)
Boeldieu, on his deathbed, and Rauffenstein discuss the changed world which will see the end of their social class along with every privilege for which it has stood.

RIGHT
Still from 'La Grande Illusion' (1937)
In a beautiful scene on Christmas Eve that overcomes religious differences, Rosenthal (Marcel Dalio), a Jew, offers the potato carving of baby Jesus to the daughter of Elsa (Dita Parlo).

(Maréchal and the German mechanic). 'If a French farmer should find himself dining at the same table as a French financier, those two Frenchmen would have nothing to say to each other... But if a French farmer meets a Chinese farmer they will find any amount to talk about.'[17] Stylistically, in *Grand Illusion*, Renoir illustrates this theme by his opening parallel between the French and German messes. This common sympathy that cuts across differences struck a chord with film-goers at the time, as it strikes a chord with audiences today.

Grand Illusion was far and away Renoir's most popular and most commercially successful film. As he wrote once, 'That blessed *Grand Illusion*! I probably owe my reputation to it...'[18] It ran for a full year in Paris and six entire months in New York when it was released. The bond between the film's characters, across barriers of language and culture, ethnicity and religion, helped to carry the film's pacifist theme in France and abroad. This was at a time when it was hoped that a reminder of the First World War and the grand illusion that it was supposed to be the war to end all wars might forestall the imminent prospect of another war. So important was this theme that the film played to acclaim at Roosevelt's White House, on the one hand, while it was branded cinematographic enemy number one by Joseph Goebbels, on the other. German antipathy for the film was not simply because of its pacifism and anti-militarism. One of the major characters is Jewish and the film's exposure of anti-Semitism is another of its important themes.

On the set of 'La Grande Illusion' (1937)
This is part of the exterior sequence in the mountains involving Maréchal and Rosenthal as they try to make their way to freedom despite the cold, their hunger and their quarrel.

'*In 1937 I made a picture named* La Grande Illusion *in which I tried to express all my deep feelings for the cause of peace... Three years later the war broke out.*'

Jean Renoir

ABOVE
Still from 'La Marseillaise' (1938)
Louis XVI (Pierre Renoir) bends to read the small print of the Brunswick Manifesto. Such small print will have large consequences with the fall of his monarchy.

RIGHT
Still from 'La Marseillaise' (1938)
Inside the Tuileries Palace, the revolutionaries systematically execute the defiant aristocrats of the old regime.

The film begins in a French mess with Lieutenant Maréchal, played by Jean Gabin, listening to a gramophone and thinking about a woman named Joséphine. In this film, as we discover, men spend most of their time thinking about women. While we never meet Joséphine, nor does Maréchal, the film's opening shot is a way of telling us that like a good love story, the whole trajectory of the film is toward the fulfilment of his desire for her and by extension for the civilian life that she represents. We know this is the goal of the film, because in its concluding sequence Maréchal has a relationship with Elsa (Dita Parlo), a German farm wife who has lost her husband and brothers to the war. The whole centre of the film in the prisoner of war camps is a means of delaying or obstructing the fulfilment of desire. The bonds the prisoners form with one another in the camps become substitute fulfilments for their real objects of desire. That is why these bonds are so infused with emotion, whether it is the group bond that the inmates feel for one another in their first prison camp, or Maréchal with Boeldieu (Pierre Fresnay), or Maréchal with Rosenthal (Marcel Dalio), or Boeldieu with Rauffenstein (Erich von Stroheim). Sometimes this substitute fulfilment is explicitly sexual, as in the justifiably memorable scene in which one soldier dresses as a woman to the wonder of all the others, or in the masquerade at the camp theatricals. The homoeroticism of these sequences is unmistakable. From the very first shot of the film, then, despite the narrative blockages along the way, we have been heading toward its concluding sequence on the mountain farm. But this sequence is still inside the war, held in suspension, as it were. Maréchal and his companion, Rosenthal, are still soldiers, even if they are dressed in civilian clothes, and they will return to their units. This sequence anticipates a civilian happiness that will not be realized until and unless the world's political powers settle on peace rather than war. The fulfilment of civilian desires would be held in suspension eight long years following the release of *Grand Illusion* on 7 June 1937.

With *Grand Illusion* Renoir perfected his characteristic style of long takes, a moving camera and considerable depth of field. In an article published in 1938, in which he summarized his career to date, he explained the benefits of deep focus cinematography: 'The more I work, the more I abandon confrontations between two actors neatly set up before the camera, as in a photographer's studio. I prefer to place my characters more freely, at different distances from the camera, and to make them move. For that I need great depth of field, and it is my feeling that this sharpness is more pleasing when it is achieved with a lens made for deep focus, rather than with a shallower lens which has been stopped down.'[19] Other familiar Renoir traits are to be found in *Grand Illusion* as well, such as the use of direct sound, or shooting through doors and windows to open up his interiors to the exterior, and vice-versa. He also begins a shot on a close-up occasionally, and then has the camera pull back to encompass the larger space and the characters within it. A telling example in *Grand Illusion* is the close-up on the little manger on Christmas Eve from which the camera slowly retreats to reveal the whole room. Once again, all of these stylistic means enable Renoir to emphasize the formative role of one's environment in one's life.

La Marseillaise (1938) is a disappointment against high expectations. It is a disappointment because it espouses political doctrine in the thin guise of fiction. While Louis XVI indulges an appetite for roast chicken following a strenuous day at the hunt, he is informed that the Parisian populace has taken the Bastille. "Is it a revolt?" "No, your majesty, it is a revolution." The date is 14 July 1789. In a field

'Louis XVI lost because he had nothing more to do at that time. The monarchy had nothing more to do. And we can even say that during revolutions, it's not the revolutionaries who win, but the reactionaries who lose. The two are very different. Even if there hadn't been a revolution, the reactionaries would have lost, would have disappeared on their own.'

Jean Renoir

somewhere in the south of France, a rake-thin peasant is apprehended because he kills a pigeon (his 'chicken') for food. Threatened with the galleys, he escapes his trial and joins other fugitives in the mountains behind Marseilles. They are helped by a priest who has his own grievances against the avarice and injustices of authority. When the châteaux of landowners and bishops burn, the fugitives leave the mountains to play their part in the revolution. The film then follows the volunteer Marseilles Battalion as they make the long trek to Paris. In the course of their journey, we meet the film's principal characters and hear their motives in support of the Revolution. Once the battalion reaches Paris, they enjoy something of its delights (new girlfriends, different cuisine, a political show with shadow-puppets) and mix with volunteers from other parts of the country. As usual, Renoir is at his best in his attention to unassuming detail, such as conversations about food (potatoes versus tomatoes), the Paris weather, or fashionable dances (by French émigrés in Coblenz). Finally, the Battalion participates in the assault on the Tuileries Palace which brings down Louis XVI, Marie Antoinette and the French monarchy on 10 August 1792. During the assault, Bomier, one of our heroes, is killed. The survivors go on to the Battle of Valmy. We have participated in the birth of the French nation.

Too much of *La Marseillaise* is scripted to conform to the political agenda of the government of the Popular Front that came to power in 1936 (but was on its way out by 1938). For example, the sympathetic treatment of the priest is an explicit acknowledgement of the so-called policy of '*la main tendue*' or open hand by which the parties of the left compromised their anti-clericalism by wooing the church. One has only to contrast this representation here with the vicious satire of the priesthood and the church in Renoir's *Le Crime de Monsieur Lange* of three years before. There, Batala, the exploiter, is disguised as a prelate to suggest that capital and clergy work hand in glove, so to speak. In addition to one's reservations about the film's subservience to domestic political agendas, one might equally have reservations about the film's accommodation to international politics. It promotes a narrow nationalism as the antidote to the rise of European fascism, a cure which is the same as the disease. That is the point of the film's strategic claim to the meaning of words like "citizen" and "nation". That is the point of its claim on the universality of the French language ("Ici on parle français,"/"French spoken here," says one sign), or of its claim to important signifiers of the Republic like the tricolour, Marianne and the 'Marseillaise' itself, all which it would recuperate from the right. That is the claim that lies behind its conclusion with the Battle of Valmy and the defeat of combined Prussian and émigré forces. All of this is to say that the battle the film engages in the name of (a) Revolution is far more about narrow ideological claims than about social, economic or cultural claims: "Revolutionaries should prefer words to battle" is one of the film's most important catchphrases.

In the film's favour, one could defend its topicality as a necessity. First of all there was the domestic situation in which the progressive hopes invested in the Popular Front were quickly unravelling under pressure to retrench on reform, even as the film was being made. Secondly, an ideology of nationalism might seem the only viable strategy given an international situation in which democratic states like France found themselves increasingly beleaguered by a fascist Europe. Unfortunately, to defend the film on these grounds is still to acknowledge that it is driven by rather obvious agendas and suffers in the consequence.

La Bête humaine (*The Human Beast*, 1938) was a huge commercial success. Based on the Zola novel, it is a disturbing film to this day. Jacques Lantier (Jean

TOP LEFT
On the set of 'La Marseillaise' (1938)
On location at Fontainebleau, which doubled for the Tuileries, Renoir can be seen giving directions behind the piled up sacks which will be used to shield the defenders.

LEFT
Still from 'La Marseillaise' (1938)
In a shot from inside the Tuileries looking out, we can see the Revolutionaries breach the gateway and flood into the courtyard.

ABOVE
Still from 'La Marseillaise' (1938)
Louison (Nadia Sibirskaïa) cradles the dying Bomier (Edmond Ardisson), her lover from the Marseilles Battalion, who has been mortally wounded in the assault on the Tuileries.

Gabin) is an engine driver who is given to unpredictable bouts of madness in which he strangles women (often in the midst of a sexual embrace). The film begins with a sensational overture in which we travel with Lantier and Pecqueux, his fireman, on board their engine of the Paris-Le Havre express. Roubaud, the station-master at Le Havre, risks a reprimand because of a disgruntled upper middle-class passenger who has arrived on the inbound train. To forestall a grievance, he sends his beautiful young wife Séverine to intercede with the influential Grandmorin on his behalf. (As played by Simone Simon, Séverine is very much the type of the *femme fatale* of film noir.) When Séverine returns from her rendezvous with Grandmorin, Roubaud beats her and accuses her of having slept with him, now and in the past. Further, because Séverine's mother was in Grandmorin's employ, there is a powerful suggestion that Séverine is Grandmorin's illegitimate daughter with whom he has therefore committed incest. In revenge, Roubaud enlists Séverine's help to murder Grandmorin on the Paris-Le Havre express. Like the other murders in Renoir's films of the 1930s, this one too is screened from our direct observation, but there is no suggestion whatsoever that it has been committed on behalf of the larger community. In fact, Cabuche, a working class character played by Renoir, who might have represented that community, is unjustly charged and imprisoned for the crime. Only Jacques Lantier, who happens to be a passenger on this particular train, knows the truth. His silence is bought by his sexual passion for Séverine. As their relationship deepens, Séverine urges Lantier to kill Roubaud. When his nerve fails, she becomes disgusted with his weakness and breaks off their relationship. The murderous tendencies of the plot and its characters come to a head when Lantier kills Séverine in a brutal scene that is intercut with a sad song about "the little heart of Ninon" which is being sung at the Railwaymen's Ball. The next morning, moving like a zombie, Lantier takes charge of the express for Paris. As the train hurtles through the countryside, he throws himself from the engine to his death.

La Bête humaine is Renoir's one, brilliant contribution to the cycle of late 1930s French works known as poetic realism. Contradictorily, their remarkable attention to the details of character and place is at the service of a moody, atmospheric style. Renoir's close observation of train travel and the culture of railway life in *La Bête humaine* is superb and convincing. At the same time, the fatalism that drives Jacques Lantier, the doom that shrouds Jean Gabin's character, is almost supernatural.

La Règle du jeu (*The Rules of the Game*, 1939) is not Renoir's most commercially successful film, not his most popular, or his most perfect aesthetically, but it is undoubtedly his greatest film.

In 1952, in the first of its ten-year polls, *Sight and Sound* magazine ranked *The Rules of the Game* tenth among the greatest films of all time. This judgement was based on critics' knowledge of an abbreviated 81 minute version only. Thereafter, with the film's reconstruction to a running time of 106 minutes, from 1962 on through the latest such poll in 2002, *The Rules of the Game* has been placed either second or third in world rankings. For the French New Wave and for François Truffaut in particular, this was a film that rewarded constant rescreening as a whole generation of film-makers went to school on the lessons it offered. The esteem in which *The Rules of the Game* is held can be gauged by the number of times it has been imitated, mined or reworked by other film-makers in sincere flattery of Renoir's achievement: *Lumière d'été* (Jean Grémillon, France, 1943), *Smiles of a Summer Night* (Ingmar Bergman, Sweden, 1955), *Réjeanne Padovani* (Denys Arcand, Canada, 1973), *The Shooting Party* (Alan Bridges, Great Britain, 1984), *Gosford Park*

ABOVE
On the set of 'La Bête humaine' (1938)
Filming trains in motion at high speed is dangerous work. Claude Renoir works behind a camera mounted on a platform attached to the locomotive.

OPPOSITE
Still from 'La Bête humaine' (1938)
A classic shot of Jean Gabin as our tainted hero Jacques Lantier, who drives the locomotive of the Paris-Le Havre express.

Still from 'La Bête humaine' (1938)
Jacques Lantier strangles Séverine (Simone
Simon), his lover, prior to stabbing her with a
paper knife.

RIGHT
Still from 'La Bête humaine' (1938)
Cabuche (Jean Renoir) is arrested for the murder
on the Paris-Le Havre express. By playing this
part, did Renoir intend to take upon himself the
weight of society's wrongfully accused?

On the set of 'La Bête humaine' (1938)
Renoir gives direction to Jean Gabin and Simone
Simon in the rail yard. The look of film noir, with
its heavy shadows and high contrast, can be
seen even in this still.

ABOVE
On the set of 'La Bête humaine' (1938)
In the film's only process shot, Lantier jumps to his suicide from the moving train. Gabin decided they had better do it this way, in the event that retakes were needed.

LEFT
On the set of 'La Bête humaine' (1938)
Filming on location in driving rain cannot have been a lot of fun. Smoke and steam rising up from the engine add to the film noir atmospherics.

(Robert Altman, USA, 2001). In short, *The Rules of the Game* is a film-maker's film, also much admired by critics and historians, but ignored by a wider public which has always preferred *Grand Illusion*.

The Rules of the Game is a comedy of manners. It is indebted to Alfred de Musset's *Les Caprices de Marianne* (1833) for some of its character types and plot devices. But above all it is indebted to Marivaux and plays like *Le Jeu de l'amour et du hasard* (1730) for its moralism in the tradition of the early 18th century and a certain cynicism about human beings in society. This is a wolf of a social film in the sheep's clothing of a morality tale. André Jurieux, a celebrated aviator, has broken Lindbergh's record for transatlantic solo flight. He is disappointed that Christine, the woman whom he loves, is not at Le Bourget airport to meet him. He blurts out his feelings to a nationwide radio audience and commits a social faux pas of such magnitude that it will eventually cost him his life in a hunting 'accident'. Christine is the wife of a Jewish Marquis, Robert de La Chesnaye, who is himself weighed down by an affair with his mistress Geneviève. In the closed world of the Parisian *haute bourgeoisie*, such adulterous liaisons are commonplace and accepted, as long as they do not become a public spectacle. The film begins by setting up an apparent contrast between the public radio over which André expresses his feelings and the private domestic spaces where Robert, Christine, Geneviève and the other upper-class characters all hear his remarks. Furthermore, André's remarks are made at night, in the dark, whereas the others listen at home, in the light. Conventionally, one might associate the former with falsehood and the latter with truth. However, the conventionality of this contrast easily collapses, like most contrasts in the film, when we recognize that André's feelings are indeed true, although public and delivered in the dark, whereas all of the other characters, except Christine, live their private lies, albeit in the light. In view of the film's subject-matter, then, truth and lies form its main both/and rather than either/or contrast, but there are other sets of terms whose meaning is no less indeterminate, such as love and friendship, reality and appearance, life and theatre, fences and rabbits, and, most critically, murder and accident. The film allows us to consider that André's death may be both a murder *and* an accident, even though the characters themselves are inclined to see it as one or the other.

This indeterminacy of meaning in the film is also conveyed by the characters' dressing up in costume during a fête at Robert's country estate and by the film's play with mistaken identities. Schumacher, the gamekeeper, thought he was shooting Octave, not André, whom he assumed was going to meet Lisette, his wife, not Christine. Stylistically, the film's brilliance lies with its overlapping dialogues and other sounds, its long takes, mobile camera and extreme depth of field. These effects allow Renoir to film two, three or four actions going on simultaneously. These actions frequently conflict with or play off one another, so that they compete for our visual and aural attention. This lack of certainty about the locus of stable meaning is what gives Octave fits, a dilemma which he expresses as "Everybody has his reasons."

The film's set piece is a hunt in which Robert's guests kill dozens of pheasants and rabbits with such violence that one has the impression that this action represents the lengths to which they would go to defend their life of privilege. That defence includes the death of André Jurieux inasmuch as the hunt clearly anticipates his end when he is said to have fallen like a rabbit. On the eve of the Second World War, the film becomes a damning portrait of a hypocritical society closed in upon

Marguerite Bussot: *"What exactly will* The Rules of the Game *be?"*
Jean Renoir: *"A precise description of the bourgeoisie of our time."*

ABOVE
On the set of 'La Règle du jeu' (1939)
Renoir is at the blackboard planning out the scenes of the film while Yvonne Bénézech, the production secretary, types directions.

OPPOSITE
Still from 'La Règle du jeu' (1939)
Robert (Marcel Dalio) and Geneviève (Mila Parely) embrace after the hunt against the backdrop of the Sologne marshes. Unfortunately for all concerned, they are observed by Christine. Everything changes after this.

ABOVE
Still from 'La Règle du jeu' (1939)
The 'danse macabre' of the skeletons among the guests during the fête suggests that the whole society is engaged in a dance of death on the eve of World War Two.

OPPOSITE
Still from 'La Règle du jeu' (1939)
Marceau (Julien Carette), the poacher, offers the rabbit with which he has been caught red-handed as a peace offering to Schumacher, the gamekeeper.

PAGES 104/105
On the set of 'La Règle du jeu' (1939)
Nora Gregor and Renoir are being lined up for a close shot on the balcony exterior of the Château de la Ferté Saint-Aubin.

itself. Although most of the film's characters are individually sympathetic, Renoir's 'exact description of the bourgeoisie of our age' (his words) condemns French society as a whole for its strict divisions of social class, its anti-Semitism and xenophobia, and its generally conservative values. In retrospect, the film seems to have been extremely prescient, even if audiences at the time were largely oblivious to what it had to say.

When the film was released to the press on 7 July 1939 and then to the general public on 8 July, its critical reception was mixed but its popular reception was largely unfavourable. The film was immediately cut to approximately 81 minutes from about 94 minutes. With the outbreak of war, first the French Government, then Vichy, and then the occupying Germans banned the film. After the war, it circulated once again in its abbreviated version. In post-war France and England *The Rules of the Game* acquired the reputation of a *film maudit*. In 1958 a company in Paris, Les Grands Films Classiques, set out to restore the film to the state of its first exhibition in July 1939. The company put together a version of the film which included material that had never been seen before and was not even part of Renoir's original montage. That is why we have a film today that runs 106 minutes and is longer than Renoir's initial release version.

Unlike *Grand Illusion*, *The Rules of the Game* cannot be said to have opened any doors for the future of Renoir's career. But two important consequences did follow from the experience, one personal and the other professional. In the course of production, Renoir severed his relationship with Marguerite and within a week of the film's premiere was in Italy with Dido Freire where he would begin a version of *La Tosca*. He had known Dido since 1927 and she had been the script girl on *The Rules of the Game*. They would journey to America together and marry there in 1944. Renoir was in Rome through the summer of 1939 and then again in the spring of 1940 until Italy entered the war in June. He scouted locations for *La Tosca*, worked on the adaptation from the Sardou play, and apparently shot the opening sequence. Whether he shot the whole of this sequence or only part of it is unclear. It does begin with five shots in which the camera tracks, pans, and tilts as it follows two mounted guardsmen on a night-time ride through Rome. The camera work and the direct sound, which pick up the advancing guardsmen and then lose them and then pick them up again, seem very much like Renoir's work. However, the film was completed by Carl Koch, Renoir's long-time assistant, so it is as much (or more) Koch's as it is Renoir's.

With the fall of France Renoir, Dido, Paul Cézanne, Jr., his wife, Renée, and their children took what belongings they could manage, including valuable paintings, joined the flood of refugees, and headed south to the Renoir family home at Les Collettes in Cagnes-sur-mer. From Cagnes as a base, with the help of Robert Flaherty and other friends, Renoir spent the balance of 1940 negotiating an exit visa which would get him and Dido to Casablanca, then Lisbon, and finally to New York on 31 December 1940. 'On the plane to Hollywood, our final destination, my wife and I tried to picture what was in store for us. I dreamed of myself installed in that paradise, with Griffith, Charlie Chaplin, Lubitsch and all the other great figures in the world-cult of the cinema.'[20]

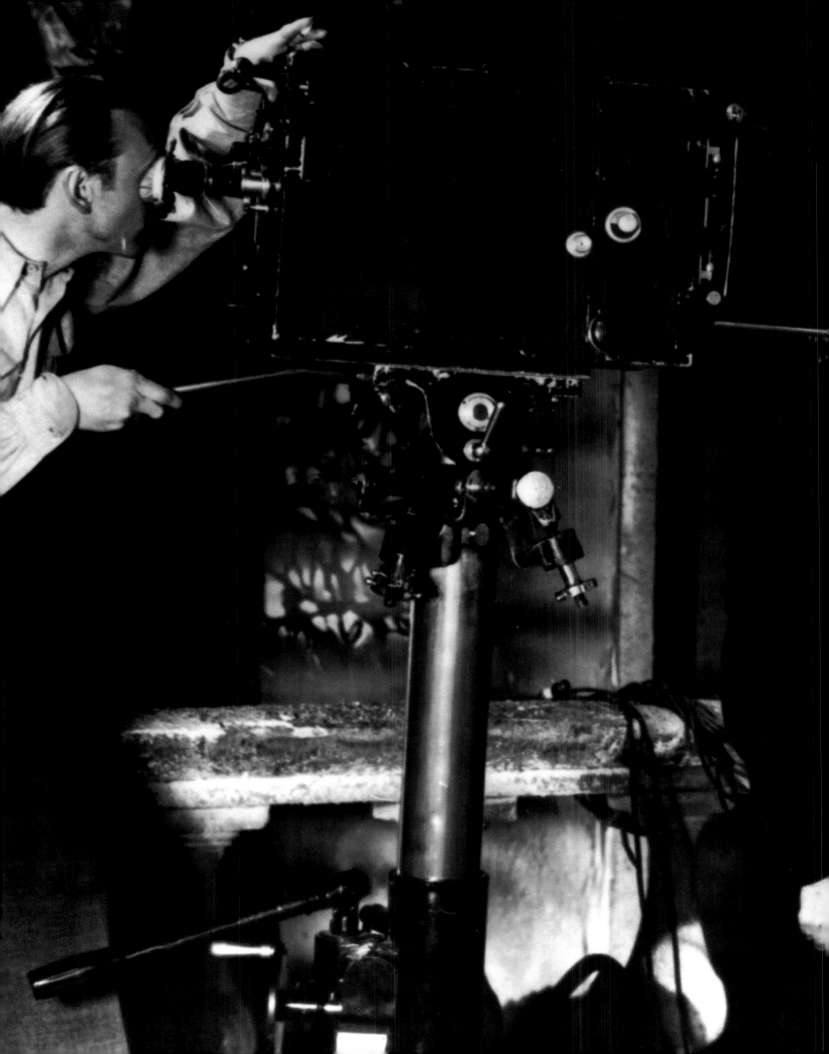

TOP
Still from 'La Règle du jeu' (1939)
The images on this double-page spread illustrate the interconnections between the major characters, despite class barriers. Robert demonstrates his mechanical warbler to Octave (Renoir). His ability to make it work has everything to do with his ability to control his emotional life.

MIDDLE
Still from 'La Règle du jeu' (1939)
Octave leans over the balustrade of the château steps, with Marceau behind, as he realizes what he has done in sending André Jurieu to his death.

BOTTOM
Still from 'La Règle du jeu' (1939)
Relationships in this film cross class barriers as Marceau, the poacher turned servant, asks Robert, the Marquis, to have a look out for Schumacher, the gamekeeper.

'Throughout the entire last part of The Rules of the Game *the camera acts like an invisible guest wandering about the salon and corridors with a certain curiosity, but without any more advantage than its invisibility.'*

André Bazin

When I made The Rules of the Game I knew where I was going. I knew the evil that gnawed at my contemporaries. My instinct guided me, my awareness of the imminent danger led me to situations and the dialogue.'

Jean Renoir

TOP
Still from 'La Règle du jeu' (1939)
Christine consoles Octave on the steps after his abortive attempt to conduct the imaginary orchestra.

MIDDLE
Still from 'La Règle du jeu' (1939)
As Christine prepares to go out for the evening, she and Lisette (Paulette Dubost) discuss whether it is possible to have a friendship with a man that does not involve romance.

BOTTOM
Still from 'La Règle du jeu' (1939)
Schumacher (Gaston Modot), the gamekeeper, tries to get free of Lisette so that he can pursue Marceau. He is out of his element inside the château.

PAGES 108/109
Location scouting for 'La Tosca' (1941)
Luchino Visconti (second left) and Renoir (right) scout locations for 'La Tosca' at Villa Adriana near Tivoli in 1939.

Hollywood
1941–1947

Renoir's sojourn in the United States and his film career there between 1941 and 1948 are far more interesting than is usually supposed. First of all, his travails with American producers and American production methods are legendary. While shooting *Swamp Water* (1941) for Darryl F. Zanuck, Renoir is reported to have expressed delight at this opportunity to work for '15th Century-Fox'. Whether apocryphal or not, the story confirms Renoir's discontent, a discontent about which he was always diplomatic, given his halting command of English. That drawback led him to encourage Anne Baxter's stand-in to 'wet [herself] a little' during the making of *Swamp Water*, when what Renoir was really after was to get her to 'wait a little' before she crossed a stream for a particular shot. Hollywood wasn't easy for a Frenchman used to '...drinking red wine and eating Brie cheese against grey Parisian vistas...'[21]

What is missing from standard accounts of Renoir's Hollywood years is any recognition of his political activism. Historians have usually supposed that when Renoir arrived in the United States he abandoned his political commitments. That does not appear to have been the case, even though Renoir never acknowledged any involvement in political affairs during the period of his American films. Many of those film personnel and artists from other cultural fields who fled Europe for America with the spread of European fascism and the rise of Nazism were left-leaning, fellow travellers like Renoir, or even avowedly Communist. Many were also Jewish, and their lives and careers were therefore doubly threatened. With the U.S. entry into the war in 1941 and with the U.S.S.R. as an ally, they were not at risk for their views. However, with the arrival of the Cold War, their politics were severely compromised and their past allegiances brought them under a cloud of suspicion. To continue to espouse a politics of the left in a climate of suspicion necessitated going underground to some extent. With the investigations of the House Committee on Un-American Activities and the anti-Communist hysteria fomented by McCarthyism in the late 1940s and 1950s, any such activity past or present made one extremely vulnerable to attack, to imprisonment, or to deportation.

Nevertheless, there was an American Popular Front of the 1940s which espoused many of the same anti-fascist, anti-racist, pro-labour causes as the French Popular Front of the 1930s, albeit transposed to United States soil. For his part, Renoir was active on behalf of the Joint Anti-Fascist Refugee Committee, the People's

Jean Renoir in New York (1956)
Renoir sticks his head out a window in New York to catch a view of the city. The Chrysler Building is in the background.

'I always did what I wanted to in Hollywood, and if I made mistakes there, I would have made them in Paris.'

Jean Renoir

ABOVE
Location scouting for 'Swamp Water' (1941)
The camera is set up on the porch of the Levas Johnson farm near Waycross, Georgia, in preparation for a location shot. Renoir is standing to the left.

LEFT
Location scouting for 'Swamp Water' (1941)
A local Georgia boy sits whittling on a porch of a general store somewhere on the edge of the Okefenokee.

OPPOSITE
Location scouting for 'Swamp Water' (1941)
Renoir peers into a murky pool on location in the Okefenokee. With the light and the reflections, this is reminiscent of the Sologne marshes where he shot 'The Rules of the Game'.

ABOVE
Still from 'Swamp Water' (1941)
Tom Keefer (Walter Brennan) prepares to club
Ben Ragan (Dana Andrews) over the head to
protect his hideout in the swamp.

RIGHT
Still from 'Swamp Water' (1941)
Jesse Wick (John Carradine) makes unwelcome
(?) advances to Hannah Ragan (Mary Howard)
on the Ragan porch while husband Thursday is
away fox hunting.

ABOVE
On the set of 'Swamp Water' (1941)
Renoir explains to Ward Bond how he wants to
choreograph the fight with Dana Andrews in
which the evil Dorson attempt to drown our hero.

LEFT
On the set of 'Swamp Water' (1941)
Renoir is in heated conversation with Anne
Baxter and Dana Andrews about how he wants
them to play a scene. Given Renoir's non-
existent English, does anybody understand?

ABOVE
On the set of 'Swamp Water' (1941)
Rafts are being used in the Okefenokee Swamp to capture some precious location footage. Despite Renoir's best efforts, the film loses something in not being able to incorporate more of the swamp.

RIGHT
On the set of 'Swamp Water' (1941)
Dana Andrews and Anne Baxter are in hysterics as Dana tries to restrain the dog 'Trouble' from getting at another member of the company being held in a cage.

On the set of 'The Amazing Mrs. Holliday' (1943)
Renoir tries to explain something to a sweet-faced Deanna Durbin. In view of her costume, we are evidently in 'China'. The camera has been prepared for a tracking shot.

'Without regretting my first American films, I know for sure that they represent nothing of my ideal.'

Jean Renoir

Educational Association, the League of American Writers, and the National Council of American-Soviet Friendship. All of these organisations were named by the U.S. Department of Justice as subversive, cultural front organisations on behalf of Communist interests. All of this activity certainly left its mark on Renoir's film work during his Hollywood years.[22]

To say that Renoir and Dido were excited about the prospect of making films in America is an understatement. As Renoir himself said, the opportunity to work in the land that produced the best of Mack Sennett, Chaplin, Stroheim, D.W. Griffith and the performers he had admired from his youth was like a dream come true. To fulfil the dream, he set about working on an adaptation of a novel by Antoine de Saint-Exupéry, wrote a script with David Flaherty, Robert's brother, and excitedly planned other projects. Alas, all for naught because, as he soon discovered, one had to prove oneself within the studio system before being trusted with one's own projects. A track record as the outstanding French film-maker of his generation carried little weight. Like many another talented émigré who arrived in California, Renoir had to start again from zero and apprentice on house films. To that end, he signed his one year contract with Twentieth Century-Fox.

From the opening shot of *Swamp Water* (1941) we are, and we are not, in familiar Renoir territory. The beginning of the film introduces us to Georgia's Okefenokee Swamp through location work with a travelling camera. The swamp itself is apparently being announced as the subject-matter of the film, something like a precursor of Robert Flaherty's *Louisiana Story* (1948). In the course of the film, Tom Keefer's (Walter Brennan's) account of his accommodation with the natural world and his belief in the sanctity of animal life sounds plausibly like Renoir, even though it was written by Dudley Nichols. Cleverly, the film does use Ben Ragan's (Dana Andrews') dog, 'Trouble', as a means of inaugurating the plot by having him lost in the swamp, and then as a way of linking various characters (Keefer and Ben, especially) as the plot develops. Keefer's daughter, Julie (Anne Baxter), is an innocent waif who is associated with animals throughout; the film's evildoers are cruel to animals. Julie is reminiscent of the innocent Virginie of *La Fille de l'eau*. However, as the film advances, the location shots become fewer and more selective and clash

BELOW
Still from 'This Land is Mine' (1943)
Albert Lory (Charles Laughton) expresses horror at the anti-Semitic 'J' for 'Jew' inked on the cheek of Edmond Lorraine (John Donat) by his classmates.

RIGHT
On the set of 'This Land is Mine' (1943)
Renoir is in conference with Walter Slezak, George Sanders and Maureen O'Hara (back to camera) on the set of the station master's office.

Still from 'This Land is Mine' (1943)
Paul Martin (Kent Smith), the saboteur, grapples with a German soldier who blocks the path of his getaway on the bridge over the rail yard.

Stills from 'This Land is Mine' (1943)
Top Left: Major von Keller (Walter Slezak) explains to Lory in his jail cell the benefits of Occupation and the good that Germany will do in the 'New World Order'. Top Right: Professor Sorel (Philip Merivale) waves to Lory in his cell as he is about to be executed by firing squad. The experience turns Lory to the side of Resistance. Above: At his trial, Lory confesses his love for Louise Martin (Maureen O'Hara) from the dock. As is often the case in Renoir's work, private and public life meet across a threshold. Right: Defiant at film's end, Lory is arrested in his classroom after reading the 'Declaration of the Rights of Man and the Citizen' to his students.

with the false note created by Twentieth Century-Fox's studio swamp with its cutaways to alligators and other 'wild life'. The sound stage dialogue and post-synchronized music and sound effects add to this false note. The idea of telling a story about straightforward country people in their own environment must have appealed to Renoir. But having to work with a stable of professional actors, however talented, and who had no particular attachment to the milieu in which the story is set, would have right away sounded another false note. In Dudley Nichols, he had a good writer, but Renoir's ignorance of English meant he had no ear for what the actors were saying or the inflections with which they said it. There are occasional moving camera shots, some shooting through doors and windows, and occasional uses of depth of field, especially around the homesteads and at the dance, but they do not seem to be deployed systematically. Finally, the story of a man, Keefer, falsely accused of murder, who successfully hides out in the Okefenokee until he is vindicated through the persistence of Ben and his dog Trouble adds up to a rather simplified moral balance sheet (replete with a few doses of religiosity). This may have been very much to mainstream American tastes but is not very consistent with the difficult, contested moral (and social) universe of Renoir's practice in 1930s France. Too many false notes.

After his frustrations with Darryl F. Zanuck at Fox, Renoir's next contract was with Universal Pictures where he was assigned to work with Deanna Durbin on a war story called *The Amazing Mrs. Holliday*. Durbin plays a resourceful young woman who rescues nine abandoned Chinese children and brings them home to San Francisco. This was a project from which he withdrew after ten weeks, pleading the incapacity brought about by (real) difficulties with the leg he had injured in the First World War. However, it is also the case that he was wholly unsympathetic to the material and to the shooting conditions: 'I am in this film as if in a bath of sugar syrup. It is slow; it is sweet, and I have the impression that it will never end.'[23] He did shoot some scenes for this film, but it is unclear which ones exactly, or even if they made it into the final cut.

Stylistically, with *This Land is Mine* (1943), Renoir departed entirely from his mature French work with its long takes, mobile camera and deep focus cinematography. The film is dominated by the prevailing practices of continuity editing, in which scenes are broken down from establishing shots to closer shots and then to an emphatic exchange of close ups, with the cutting dependent upon the standard repertoire of eye-line matches and matches on action. Alexander Sesonske

ABOVE
On the set of 'This Land is Mine' (1943)
Renoir and Eugène Lourié, his set designer, share a laugh between friends. Lourié had dressed most of Jean's films throughout the 1930s. He wrote about their collaboration in 'My Work in Films' (1985).

BELOW LEFT
Still from 'This Land is Mine' (1943)
In a shot not included in the film, Lory tenderly watches his mother (Una O'Connor) asleep in a chair.

BELOW RIGHT
Still from 'This Land is Mine' (1943)
A second shot missing from the film shows Lory looking in on George Lambert (George Sanders), Louise, her brother Paul, and his girl friend Julie (Nancy Gates).

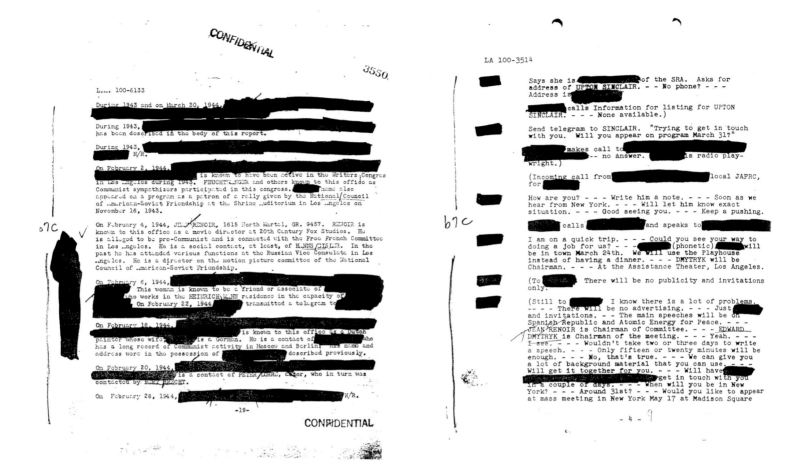

Pages from Jean Renoir's FBI file

Files kept by the FBI reveal a great deal about Renoir's political activity in the United States during the 1940s. These files still contain information that apparently needs to be suppressed. Renoir associated with a lot of people who were followed, recorded, jailed and blacklisted.

has reported in detail on Renoir's reluctant abandonment of his preferred style of shooting.[24]

In terms of its subject matter, however, *This Land is Mine* is much closer to home. The film was written and produced by Renoir with Dudley Nichols as an independent film for R.K.O. The idea was to explain to American audiences what it is like to live in an occupied country in wartime. That country is obviously France, although it is never identified as such in the film. The film's allusions to rights for women, unionized workers and a 40-hour week are clear references to gains made by the Popular Front in France that were lost under Vichy and the German Occupation. When the film was shown in France after the war, it was roundly criticized for being soft on Vichy and naïve about the Occupation. Those judgements seem unfair to a film which exposes the reality of anti-Semitism, the seductions of Nazism and the moral price of collaboration.

The asexual, slow-footed, mama's boy Albert Lory is a school-teacher in a town under the Occupation. Terrified of air raids, mocked by his students, he is secretly in love with his neighbour and fellow school-teacher, Louise Martin. She is engaged to George Lambert, who manages the railway station and acquiesces in the German presence in their town. That presence is convincingly represented by Major von Keller, an articulate, well-educated man who reads the classics and is very persuasive at rationalizing necessity on behalf of the "New World order". The film's plot turns on the discovery that the school principal, Professor Sorel, has been producing an underground newspaper and that Louise's brother, Paul, has been bombing motorcades and sabotaging supply trains. Hostages are taken in retaliation, and they include Lory and Sorel. Mrs. Lory observes Paul returning from a mission and

Gardens? - - - Spanish Refugee Committee. - - - Wires
are out. - - - Like to have you. Will communicate
with you on that.

(To ████ He might, if RENOIR pushes him. - - -
Will call RENOIR. - - - You call RENOIR and give him
the stuff for speech.

I'll call RENOIR and have him work on ████

████ calls DRexel 7261 -- local JAFRC -- speaks
to

Call Embassy Auditorium. See if available for March
25. - - - Place call to ████ (believed to be
████. - - - Remind him about ████
(an entertainer). - - - We are leaving hotel.

Mentions a man named ████ who is "his man in New York."

████ calls EXposition 1356 -- First Unitarian
Church of Los Angeles, 2936 West Eighth Street,

████ - - - This is ████ - - - Hello, ████
Just got message. - - - I am leaving on 12:01 train.
Glad to see you and ████ - - - She comes up on 24th.
(CURIE) - - - Hope you've gotten your things straightened
up.

(To ████ He's really a good guy. - - - They really
did a good job on him.

At 10:55 ████ and ████ departed from the room.

b7c

- 5 -

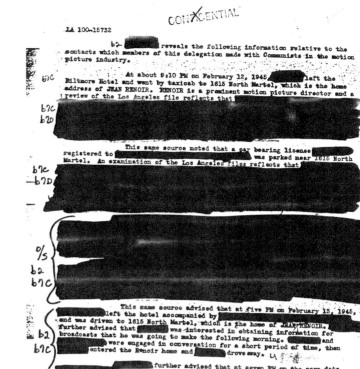

Pages from Jean Renoir's FBI file
In 1943, Renoir directed a political spectacle at
the Shrine Auditorium in Los Angeles for the
National Council of American-Soviet Friendship.
The FBI has to be considered one of the world's
unsuspected archives. But for its diligence, we
might have no record of what was formerly an
unknown work by Renoir.

ABOVE
Still from 'The Southerner' (1945)
Sam (Zachary Scott, right) and Nona (Betty Field), with Grandma (Beulah Bondi) in the foreground survey the damage to their homestead caused by torrential rains and flooding.

RIGHT
Still from 'The Southerner' (1945)
Jotty Tucker (Jay Gilpin) looks for approval before sampling some of those black raspberries.

reports this to George Lambert, who then tells von Keller. Albert is released. In the meantime, Paul is pursued and killed, leading George to commit suicide out of remorse. However, when Albert is discovered bending over George's body, he is suspected of murder and returned to jail. Major von Keller accepts Lory's innocence, but before he appears in court to be exonerated Albert observes Professor Sorel's execution from his jail cell. Shocked by the reality of Nazi brutality, he uses the occasion of his trial to denounce the Occupation and those who profit from it. The (French) court is so moved by his eloquence that he is freed, whereupon he returns to his classroom to receive the admiration of his students and the affections of Louise. He is arrested by the Germans while reading the Declaration of the Rights of Man to his class. What he leaves behind is the legacy of resistance.

This Land is Mine was an important film for Renoir, not only because it provided the opportunity to speak out about the recent betrayal of his homeland, of its democratic practices and its progressive social policies, but also because its views were consistent with the politics that he continued to espouse in America. Renoir was a quiet, and not so quiet, supporter of the American Popular Front of the 1940s and *This Land is Mine* expressed a timely opposition to racism and anti-Semitism, to collaboration with an immoral authority and to naming names, even before some of those causes became as public as they would be toward the end of the decade.

On 16 November 1943, Renoir staged and directed a work which was entirely unknown until very recently. On that date he mounted an elaborate political rally in the Shrine Auditorium in Los Angeles on behalf of the National Council of American-Soviet Friendship. The purpose was to mark the tenth anniversary of diplomatic relations between the two nations. This spectacle involved a film presentation designed to show parallels between the American and Soviet people, as well as a cantata written for the occasion, along with speeches, songs and readings. Eugène Lourié, Renoir's preferred art director, first in France from 1933 on, and later in America, was responsible for the art direction here as well. Renoir also served on committees, visited the Soviet consulate in Los Angeles, and wrote and delivered radio broadcasts on behalf of this organisation. None of this activity would have endeared him to the American right-wing, the anti-Communists and red-baiters who would lead the witch hunts of the late 1940s and early 1950s.

Salute to France (1944) is a minor film, seldom seen, commercially unavailable, to which Renoir's specific contribution has to be deduced. It was made as a commissioned work for the Office of War Information and shot in the Fox-Movietone Studios in New York. The purpose of the film was to explain France's current predicament under the Occupation and to acquaint U.S. and Allied soldiers with French customs in advance of a probable European invasion. The film was completed in March and April of 1944, six weeks or so before the D-Day landings of 6 June. Claude Dauphin, Garson Kanin and Burgess Meredith, play Jacques, Joe and Tommy, respectively, three Allied soldiers. Their conversation about France on the deck of a troop ship is intercut with found war footage and scenes illustrative of French daily life (in which they play the numerous civilian parts). In addition to its anti-collaborationist, pro-Resistance stand, the film's strength is its strong internationalist theme. There are accounts that the original cut of the film was an ambitious 90 minutes before it was twice edited down.

Like the opening of *Swamp Water*, the opening of *The Southerner* (1945) promises much, and in this case it delivers a great deal more. We are in the middle of a vast, sun-beaten cotton field somewhere in Texas. Cotton pickers under straw hats

'I don't believe that responsibility in an author ever worked. I don't believe that any author ever did any good because he was feeling a responsibility. I believe some authors instinctively feel a certain love for the human being, and they will do a lot of good, I hope. And some of the ones don't, and that's all.'

Jean Renoir

Still from 'The Southerner' (1945)
Contrary to the spirit of neighbourliness, Sam and Devers (J. Carroll Naish) fight over Sam's request for fresh water and milk for his family.

ABOVE
Still from 'The Southerner' (1945)
Sam holds aloft a fish he has caught
barehanded. This would make one good meal for
the hungry Tucker clan.

RIGHT
Still from 'The Southerner' (1945)
More important than the fish, however, is access
to fresh water from Devers' well and the
occasional cup of milk from his cow. Devers is
not interested in bartering for the fish.

On the set of 'The Southerner' (1945)
Everybody, including Renoir, is standing in the
swollen San Joaquin river to get the shots of the
aftermath of the flood as Sam and Tim try to
rescue the cow.

bend in the long rows. Black hands and black faces, white hands and white faces fill huge bags and carry them to the tally-man. Poor blacks and poor whites share their common economic hardship as indentured labour to a large grower. In one row Uncle Pete Tucker feels faint and succumbs to a weak heart, but not before urging his nephew Sam to work the land for himself. The film's story, to which William Faulkner contributed without credit, becomes the uphill battle of Sam, his wife Nona, Grandma Tucker, and kids Daisy and Jotty to raise their own subsistence crop as tenant farmers.

The location work is convincing, especially in its evocation (but not imitation) of dustbowl photographers like Walker Evans or Dorothea Lange. There are powerful images of the cotton workers' shanties, the borrowed truck piled high with the Tuckers' meagre belongings when they first arrive at their homestead, or their shack of a house with its fallen porch stuck next to a dead tree in an open field. Excellent performances by Zachary Scott as Sam, especially, and by J. Carroll Naish as his surly, uncooperative neighbour also go a long way towards lending conviction to the subject matter. None other than James Agee commended Renoir for the film's documentary qualities and the authenticity of Scott's acting.

The film succeeds through its well-observed details of gesture and speech, dress and decor, which Renoir seems to have got right as its story unrolls through the seasons of a full year. One thinks of the scene in which Sam wordlessly rolls Nona a cigarette or the shots of them sleeping up against each other outside in the early summer heat. The relationship between Sam and Nona is certainly one of the film's strengths, as we see them working together in the field ("We done all that ourselves") or touching each other with hands, shoulders, arms, when close. This warmth between them condenses the film's theme about the desirability and the necessity of human bonds, of "folks sticking together", in Sam's words. About the worst condition one could give into is that of failing to help others. That is why Devers' failure at "neighbourliness" in refusing to lend Sam milk or vegetables for Jotty's "spring sickness" (pellagra) is a grievous moral as well as social flaw. Devers has been stunted by his own past hardships as a tenant farmer when he lost crops to nature's unpredictability and children and a wife to disease. Devers is the test of Sam's inner and outer strength, the condition into which he must not fall, the failure that he must rise above. The country, work on the land, is contrasted in the film with city life and work in a factory. Sam's cousin Tim is big-hearted, but it is clear that seven dollars a day in a factory is the price of alienating labour and Sam will have none of it. The film avoids the risks of sentimentality that come with a story built around a family and its hardships. Buffeted by human and natural disaster, the family's resilience and their faith in one another carries them through to an ending which offers the potential for success but not its promise.

From the situated environment of *The Southerner*, we are back in the studio with *The Diary of a Chambermaid* (1946). The film is a period adaptation of a 19th-century novel by Octave Mirbeau, a writer who had known Pierre-Auguste in Paris when Jean was a little boy. This was a project that Renoir had wanted to undertake for a long time, perhaps as early as the period of his first sound films, and again in 1938 after he finished *La Marseillaise*. Had he made it then, perhaps he would not have made *The Rules of the Game*. Like *The Rules of the Game*, *The Diary of a Chambermaid* is set in a château amidst a crumbling upper-class family seemingly isolated from the rest of the world. The plot here, too, involves its servant class (valet, chambermaid, scullery maid), a love triangle, and similar settings (a below

TOP
Still from 'The Diary of a Chambermaid' (1946)
Captain Mauger (Burgess Meredith) demonstrates his taste for edible flowers to a sceptical Celestine (Paulette Goddard).

ABOVE
Still from 'The Diary of a Chambermaid' (1946)
The Captain endeavours to explain to Celestine how he came to strangle his pet squirrel in the heat of passion. Tellingly, they are shot through the bars of the cage.

OPPOSITE
On the set of 'The Diary of a Chambermaid' (1946)
Renoir gives Paulette Goddard hands-on lessons in how to wring clothes like a real chambermaid. Was he remembering the household full of women of his childhood?

ABOVE
Still from 'The Diary of a Chambermaid' (1946)
A defiant Celestine gets dressed in her best clothes while the timid housemaid Louise (Irene Ryan) looks on.

RIGHT
Production sketch for 'The Diary of a Chambermaid' (1946)
Dorothea Holt Redman penned this production sketch. Note the fluidity of the lines and imagined textures in keeping with the period idea of the film.

stairs kitchen, a garden, a greenhouse). *The Diary of a Chambermaid* owes something to *Catherine* as well, Renoir's first film, especially in their common endings, with the union in a railway carriage between the upper-class male and the serving girl-chambermaid on their way to a new life. The extent to which Renoir intended to recall his earlier films remains to be seen. What is certain is that the portrait of society in *The Diary of a Chambermaid*, and even of individual moral worth, is far more scathing. The characters in *The Rules of the Game* may be confused, contradictory, complacent, its society hell-bent toward disaster, but we still find them sympathetic and their world worth redeeming.

In *The Diary of a Chambermaid*, Joseph, the valet, is a cold-blooded killer ("He's an undertaker," says Celestine, the chambermaid of the film's title), who is scheming to make off with the Lanlaire family silver. He is able to enlist Celestine's help for a time because he correctly points out that they are two of a kind. Her behaviour and Paulette Goddard's performance give us reason to believe him. That she should fall sincerely in love with the tubercular George Lanlaire and leave with him at film's end is not wholly convincing unless we can set aside her complicity with Joseph and her own scheming to escape her station. The Lanlaire family is staunchly anti-Republican and that they should be brought down on 14 July as Joseph attempts to make off with the silver is fitting. However, Joseph is killed by a Republican mob in the village as he disrupts their Bastille Day celebrations. If this is an allegory of France's transition from wartime to post-war life, is the extra-judicial Republican mob any better than the tyrannical Vichyite social family that it succeeds? Or is the film in some way a gloss on Renoir's American experience, in which he wanted to show that the republican spirit of the people was not afraid to turn against the tyranny and right-wing isolationism of the few if it served the collective good?

Renoir's last American film was his most frustrating. Renoir began shooting *The Woman on the Beach* at the beginning of February 1946 and the film was released in June 1947. During those sixteen months, the film was severely cut and re-cut and whole sequences re-shot.

The Woman on the Beach is Peggy Butler (Joan Bennett), who passes much of her time in and around a wrecked naval vessel that was thrown up on the sand during the war. She is unhappily married to Tod (Charles Bickford), once a painter of some renown, whom she inadvertently blinded in a drunken passion. Tod holds Peggy close, possessively close, taking advantage of her guilt and his dependence. He has also kept some very valuable paintings which she would like him to sell. However, the film's story belongs as much or more to Lt. Scott Burnett (Robert Ryan) of the U.S. Coast Guard. His ship was sunk during the war and he suffers from a debilitating nightmare in which he sees himself falling through the waves to the ocean floor, then walking forward to meet his fiancée, only to have his underwater dream burst into flames as they are about to embrace.

What is different and therefore interesting about *The Woman on the Beach* as a Renoir film is that it is obviously a psychological tale, this from a film-maker who more than once expressed his loathing for any psychology in the cinema. The effect here is in part due to the film's affinities with film noir, evident from the nature of the story, the casting, and some of its atmospheric effects (rain, fog), although not from its settings or the lighting. Further, *The Woman on the Beach* has the sparest décors of any Renoir film, but is nevertheless heavily symbolic (water, dreams, a wrecked ship, blindness, paintings, fire). Once again, one regrets not having the film that Renoir initially shot and edited, but in what remains there is the story of two

Still from 'The Diary of a Chambermaid' (1946)
In the greenhouse during his fight with George, Joseph, the valet (Francis Lederer) pulls out the long needle he uses to kill geese. Celestine's horror is justified.

Still from 'The Woman on the Beach' (1947)
A production still from the opening dream
sequence with Lt. Scott Burnett (Robert Ryan)
advancing to meet Eve Geddes (Nan Leslie) on
the sea floor.

ABOVE
Still from 'The Woman on the Beach' (1947)
Peggy Butler (Joan Bennett) and Scott Burnett meet on the beach by the abandoned navy wreck. She is gathering firewood; he offers her warmth.

LEFT
Still from 'The Woman on the Beach' (1947)
Peggy looks slyly over her shoulder at a disappearing Scott while her blind husband, Tod Butler (Charles Bickford), looks straight ahead.

BELOW
Still from 'The Woman on the Beach' (1947)
Peggy and Tod have an abusive relationship that will only be overcome when they have both put the past behind them.

RIGHT
Still from 'The Woman on the Beach' (1947)
Peggy tries to save a valuable painting that Tod is about to destroy. The fire that consumes his paintings frees them from the prison of their past.

(sexually) impotent men who both have to be released from the prison of their pasts by a *femme fatale* who acts as a catalyst.

Lt. Burnett is drawn to Peggy and Tod knows it. What Burnett does not know is that despite everything Peggy and Tod are bound to each other in a longstanding love-hate relationship. Burnett tries (unconsciously) to kill Tod by leading the blind painter along a cliff's edge, and then a second time (consciously) by taking him fishing in a storm and trying to sink their boat. The latter experience finally drives Tod to realize that even at the risk of losing Peggy he must fully acknowledge his blindness by destroying the paintings that represent the visible evidence of his and their past life. Tellingly, one of these paintings, the best work he has ever done, he says, is a nude portrait of Peggy. In setting fire to his paintings, he has not only set himself free, he has set Peggy free from the hold he has over her so that they can affirm their love for each other unmediated by the paintings and the traumatic history they record. What is not so clear is the fate of Lt. Burnett. However, the film's last shot is a dissolve which shows fire being consumed by water, rather than fire overcoming water as it had in his nightmare. We might assume that Burnett, too, has been released from his trauma and is free to embrace his fiancée and his future.

The Woman on the Beach spelled the end of Renoir's American career, but not because his work there was a complete critical or commercial disaster. Despite numerous setbacks to do with the Hollywood system of production and the frustrations of studio work, Renoir endeavoured to go on working in the United States. However, he was stonewalled in his efforts to raise money or launch new projects. There is some possibility that Renoir's name appeared on producer and studio 'greylists' as unemployable because of his political associations in and out of the cinema during the 1940s. *The Woman on the Beach* was released four and a half months before the climate of fear that surrounded the subpoena before the House Committee on Un-American Activities of 19 witnesses from the film industry in October 1947. Some of the famous Hollywood Ten who appeared and some of the nine who did not were Renoir's friends and colleagues. For example, Renoir's composer on *The Woman on the Beach* was Hanns Eisler, an extremely talented musician who was 'voluntarily deported' in February 1948 for his Communist affiliations. It was time to move on and take the conversation elsewhere.

On the set of 'The Woman on the Beach' (1947)
Renoir chats with Joan Bennett while an
attendant bathes her feet.

International Film-maker 1950–1969

In 1952 Renoir wrote two short essays in which he testified to the profound change in direction that his life and work had undergone: 'I Know Where I'm Going' ('On me demande...') and 'Something Happened to Me' ('Quelque chose m'est arrivé'). No doubt precipitated by the knowledge that he would never work in Hollywood again, he appears to have abjured politics once and for all and embraced a more purely cultural solution to the problems of human affairs. India and the making of *The River* in 1949-50 proved to be the transformative experience needed to crystallize this change in direction. Renoir at last fulfilled in body as well as spirit the course of his longstanding internationalist convictions and became a citizen of the world. From India, he would find his way to Italy, France, Austria, and back to France to make his last films.

The critic André Bazin once made the case that Renoir's potential as a film-maker could only be realized with the arrival of sound cinema and, conversely, that sound cinema needed the presence of Renoir to realize its full potential. He might have said the same thing with respect to the arrival of colour, and of Renoir's spectacular use of it in his films of the 1950s and 1960s. However, the advent of colour in Renoir's work, unlike the advent of sound, did not have the benefit of bringing him closer to external reality, but of driving him away from it. If the tension between appearance and reality or theatre and life in his films of the 1930s always concluded by favouring reality, in the 1950s the balance tipped in favour of theatre in what looks like a return to some of the emphases of his silent period. Renoir once and for all largely sacrificed the sense of place that was so much a part of his realist aesthetic of the 1930s, an aesthetic that was compromised by the demands of Hollywood in the 1940s. He also avoided any contemporary issues during the 1950s, whether political or social (as one example, the French presence in Algeria). This indicates how far he has come from his period of engagement in the 1930s and from his commitments during the 1940s.

He elected instead to set his films in a world of artifice (*The River* notwithstanding) and period subject-matter (*The River* excepted). *The Golden Coach* (1953), *French Cancan* (1955) and *Elena and Her Men* (1956) are set quite literally in theatrical milieu, but about all four of these 1950s films there is a visible sense of artifice, in their dazzling colour palettes, in the acting styles, and in their devotion to spectacle. Suddenly, in Renoir's work, the actual materiality of cinema is at the

Jean Renoir at Chez Albert Lewin (1971)
Renoir reaches out while he speaks, so that his hand seems to cover the breast of the seated figure in 'Le Cri' by Paul Delvaux.

'Today, the new being that I am realises that this is not the time for sarcasm and that the only thing that I can bring to this illogical, irresponsible and cruel universe is my love.'

Jean Renoir

ABOVE
Still from 'The River' (1951)
Renoir wanted to incorporate documentary impressions of India into his fiction film. The movement of the boats involved in everyday commerce on the river is one example.

RIGHT
Still from 'The River' (1951)
Valerie (Adrienne Corri) does her best to get Captain John (Thomas Breen) to overcome the antisocial feelings that he has built up because of the loss of his leg in the war. Thomas Breen had also lost a leg during the war.

oreground of our attention in a way that it never was before. As one of the arts of performance, cinema itself is on display.

Renoir's first colour film was the first Technicolor film made wholly in India and one of the first films in the history of motion pictures to record sound on magnetic tape. Martin Scorsese has described it as one of the two most beautiful colour films ever made and the first film to introduce him to a foreign culture. *The River* was produced by Kenneth McEldowney, a Hollywood florist, who shared Renoir's love for the Rumer Godden novel of the same title. She was an Anglo-Indian and the benefit of her experience was indispensable to the writing of the script and to shooting on location. Propitiously, shooting began on 29 December 1949, on the Feast of Saraswati, the Goddess of the Arts and Artists, near the banks of the Hoogli River, about 25 miles from Calcutta. Altogether, Renoir and Dido spent five months in India, first shooting the film and then in Madras at the home of Radha, one of the film's stars. To say that the experience changed Renoir's life is an understatement.

This experience and his impression of India found its way into *The River* first of all through a strategic division in the film between the white, colonial English family and their friends, on the one hand, and the film's views of Indian customs and Hindu ritual, on the other. The film's narrative fiction concerns this family and the coming of age of Harriet, the adolescent daughter, and her friends Valerie, another English girl, and Melanie (Radha), their friend and neighbour, who is the child of an Indian mother and an Irish father. The story of *The River* is the story of Harriet's emerging (romantic) desires, told in flashback with the aid of the voice-over of the mature Harriet, who tends to be critical of her self-absorbed ugly duckling of a younger self. The catalyst for this burst of desire in the three girls is Captain John, a young American, bitter at the loss of his leg in the war, who has arrived for a visit (perhaps vainly looking for a country of one-legged men). When Captain John chooses Valerie, like the Paris of Greek myth awarding the prized apple to the greatest

LEFT
Still from 'The River' (1951)
Melanie (Radha Sri Ram) dances the part of the Lady Radha for her betrothed in the part of the Lord Krishna at their wedding ceremony.

BELOW
Still from 'The River' (1951)
Harriet, our narrator, tells a story in flashback of the cycle of birth and renewal. Here two village women make an offering in the river.

beauty, and when Harriet's little brother dies from a cobra bite (the snake in the garden of the family's Eden), Harriet is plunged into despair and attempts suicide in the river. What she learns by, in a sense, dying and being reborn out of the river is acquiescence to the endless cycle of creation and destruction which is the meaning of the ever-flowing river itself and of life and ritual in India altogether.

If the film's coming-of-age narrative is casually plotted (and its dialogue often very weak), that is because there is a whole documentary side to the film which records a Westerner's impressions of India. The narrative belongs to the colonialists; the spectacle belongs to India. Care is taken to document something of the life of India at work and at leisure on the river, the temples and their long flights of stairs running to the water's edge, festivals like Diwali (the festival to mark the beginning of winter), or innocent pleasures like kite-flying. The separation between story and document reminds us that these Westerners (including the film-maker himself) are in India but never of it. They are forever on the outside looking in. The one character who bridges fiction and documentary, west and east, Christianity and Hinduism, is Melanie, a character who is caught between two lives, two places, two cultures and who has to learn to be at home in both. Melanie is the one for whom questions of

ABOVE
Still from 'The River' (1951)
Bogey (Richard Foster), observed by his friend Kanu (Nimai Barik), squats under another tree as he attempts to charm the cobra. This is the tree of death.

LEFT
Still from 'The River' (1951)
Trees have a special place in 'The River'. Valerie, Harriet (Patricia Walters) and Melanie have been playing on the swing beneath the tree of life in the family's garden.

OPPOSITE
Still from 'The River' (1951)
Valerie looks on in the village marketplace as a snake charmer spirits a cobra out of its basket. The moment is premonitory, as we soon discover.

Still from 'The River' (1951)
Captain John makes his way up the gang plank
of a boat on the river at night to console Harriet
after her attempted suicide following Bogey's
death.

On the set of 'The River' (1951)
Everything is set for the filming of this night-time sequence of the festival of Diwali, the Hindu festival of light that marks the beginning of winter.

'I think that it's a mistake, for example, to make a film in Provence that is supposed to take place in Paris. One should make Provençal films in Provence and Parisian films in Paris.'

Jean Renoir

ABOVE
On the set of 'The River' (1951)
The crew prepares for the film's last scene on the balcony by the river. While cows graze in the foreground, the sound crew is under the parasol in the middleground.

RIGHT
On the set of 'The River' (1951)
Renoir gets a military escort in the front seat of an Indian army jeep. Is this how he got to work everyday?

ABOVE
On the set of 'The River' (1951)
Everything is ready to roll on the film's last few shots with Radha, Harriet and Valerie. The camera will tilt up from them to look out across the river.

LEFT
On the set of 'The River' (1951)
Thomas Breen at kerbside is either rehearsing his lines or trying to explain the meaning of life to a docile listener.

ABOVE
Still from 'The Golden Coach' (1954)
The commedia dell'arte perform for a tough
audience of indigenous peoples at their first
performance in the New World of colonial Peru.
The theatre, and the blurring between reality and
fiction, are recurring themes in Renoir's films.

RIGHT
Still from 'The Golden Coach' (1954)
The Viceroy (Duncan Lamont) takes off his wig to
impress Camilla (Anna Magnani) with his
informality.

identity (national, cultural, religious, ethnic) are the most difficult to negotiate. In that respect, she is our model for the film's transnational vision and its true protagonist, not Harriet. Melanie's situation anticipates the future that is ours today inasmuch as she belongs to both a local and a global world.

It is Melanie who advises "consent" rather than confrontation as the remedy to one's lot in life, advice that Harriet, Valerie and Captain John in his bitterness have all to heed. One has the impression that the European characters belong to a culture whose values of ceaseless struggle and headlong progress are suspect. Most importantly, it is Melanie who belongs to the film's European story world but who alone is able to cross over into its documentary, Indian world. In the film's key sequence, Harriet writes a story in her diary which we see performed with Melanie playing the part of the Lady Radha in a dance of courtship with her new husband Anil as the Lord Krishna. This glorious spectacle of the dance is the centre-piece of the film because Harriet here projects her own romantic desires into a state of being that satisfies the condition of art and/or ritual by temporarily resolving life's turmoil. We can no longer tell 'the dancer from the dance'. Renoir has no less an expectation that his film, *The River*, will accomplish as much.

The Golden Coach (1953), 'a fantasy in the Italian style', was another first as a colour film. It was the first major Italian production to be shot in Technicolor. The film was shot in Rome on the sound stages at Cinecittà in early spring 1952 in three language versions, English, French and Italian. Only the first of these was acknowledged by Renoir as the correct version. The actors were British, American and Italian and all of them were dubbed in each of the film's three languages in turn, as was customary in Italian studio film-making. For Renoir, who once famously said that dubbing was akin to a heretical belief in the duality of the soul, one imagines that the absence of direct sound for all of the voices in each version must have been extremely painful.[25] Unfortunately, the result is sometimes painful, especially when the dialogue seems disembodied (literally), or when the thickness of an accent is almost impenetrable. However, such discomforts serve as a reminder that Renoir's sense of artifice is a construction, not at all a falsehood, and that if it is to succeed we must believe in it every bit as much we might be asked to believe in the most realistic of on-location environments.

What inspires audience belief in *The Golden Coach* are its two stars, one of whom is Anna Magnani, who plays Camilla, who plays the part of Columbine in the *commedia dell'arte* theatre performed by a troupe of Italian players who come to 18th-century Spanish, colonial Peru in search of an audience and their fortune. The film's other star attraction is its sets, its breathtaking decors, which are filmed in such a way as to maximize their theatrical function. We are shown rooms within rooms, like nested boxes, or rooms beyond rooms, like a hall of mirrors, both tactics reminiscent of *The Rules of the Game*. Or we are shown two rooms side by side to create one playing space, or else a single room divided to create two playing spaces. Against the pull of depth, three rooms are arranged laterally, across which the camera and the action track in parallel. Once again, all of this ingenuity puts the resources of cinema on display as much as it does the theatre. There are moments of brilliance when the film's two stars come together, such as the scene comprised of a single shot in which Camilla attends a bullfight whose entire (invisible) drama is played out on her face as the camera pulls slowly back from its initial close-up. Renoir took excellent advantage in this scene and elsewhere of the talents of Magnani as an actor 'famous for her portrayal of stormy emotion'.[26]

'Personally, I love to improvise. Improvisation often helps to better adapt the idea of a scene to the personality of an actor, to the character of a set, of a landscape or of a prop, the meaning of which one sometimes only discovers at the last moment on the set. But this kind of improvisation is only possible when it applies to the improvement of something already existing, a kind of basis; in other words, if it is a modification of the shape, not the idea. When improvisation handles the actual invention of the story, I consider it bad.'

Jean Renoir

Still from 'The Golden Coach' (1954)
Camilla steps down from her golden coach as she arrives at the palace amidst much fanfare. She will disavow the world and give the coach to the Church.

ABOVE
Still from 'The Golden Coach' (1954)
Camilla arrives at the palace with the Bishop (Jean Debucourt) to whom she will make the gift of the coach. She will renounce her lovers in favour of the stage.

OPPOSITE TOP
On the set of 'The Golden Coach' (1954)
In this photo by Robert Capa, Renoir directs Anna Magnani's reactions amidst the crowd at the bullfight scene. The entire course of the fight is recorded in her facial expressions.

OPPOSITE BOTTOM
Still from 'The Golden Coach' (1954)
A long shot of the bullfight arena with the victorious Ramon (Riccardo Rioli) surrounded by a sea of hats.

Camilla/Columbine is desired by three men: Felipe, who becomes a soldier in the colonial wars against the Indians; the Viceroy of Peru, who has ordered the golden coach of the title for his pleasure, but which he gives to Camilla; and, Ramon, a vainglorious bullfighter. Each is plagued by jealousy; each wants Camilla for himself alone. The film opens with a curtain going up and closes with it going down. Like the mirrored effect produced by the multiple rooms that make up the sets, the action in between presents us with a dizzying *mise en abîme* of life within theatre within life within theatre without end. Camilla poses the question of the film: "Where does the theatre end and life begin?" If the question has no answer, that is because the boundaries between the one and the other are entirely fluid (this is not quite the same thing as indistinguishable). Public life and private life, court, church and military foray are all conducted on terms that approximate theatre. The serious intrigues of court are a burlesque. A bullfight ring is another stage on which an actor gambles with his mortality to the thrill of the crowd.

The theatre of life, however, is a great deal messier than the life of the theatre and merits no applause. Indians die to satisfy the European greed for the "treacherous" gold or to build a coach that will gratify personal vanity, become a symbol of State power, or carry the Church's last sacrament to the condemned. Camilla eventually renounces her three suitors, renounces life (insofar as this is possible in such a vertiginous film), renounces her desire to be an agent in the world, renounces worldly possessions, including the coach ("Where gold commands, laughter vanishes"), and concedes that only on the stage is it possible to find happiness for a couple of hours. If one misses life, if one misses one's suitors "a little", as Camilla admits, her consolation must be the applause that every actor needs as evidence of "contact with an audience".

While it seems likely that Renoir hoped success with *The Golden Coach* would provide him an entrée to French film-making, the French version was generally disliked. Consequently, his homecoming was delayed more than two years until he was given the opportunity to shoot *French Cancan* in the late fall of 1954. *French Cancan* was a frankly commercial project, but Renoir turned it to good account by rediscovering something of his roots in Montmartre, albeit through theatre and painting rather than through direct, realist depiction of 'the soil that nourished them', or of the 'grey Parisian vistas' that he had memorialized in his black and white films of the 1930s. He also helped his cause on *French Cancan* by renewing his relationship with old friends and colleagues like Jean Gabin, Gaston Modot, Max Dalban, Valentine Tessier, Max Douy and Georges Cravenne, all of whom he engaged on the film.

One evening, in the late 1880s, while slumming in Montmartre with his mistress and some friends, the impresario Danglard (Ziegler, in real life), played by an aging Gabin, is inspired to create a great music hall, the Moulin Rouge. This palace is to be the centre of popular artistic and fashionable social life for all of Paris. Danglard's innovation will be the creation of a new dance based on the working-class *chahut* and which will be called the "French Cancan" (because it sounds exotic). With this attention to the cancan's popular origins, the film collapses any pretentious distinctions between art and entertainment. Danglard chooses Nini, a little laundress, both to be his new mistress and to lead his chorus of cancan dancers. While we know that art will eventually triumph over love and theatre over life, as it did in *The River* and *The Golden Coach*, what the film manages to set before us in the way of blockages to its end are not only the personal jealousies of the various characters but

also an astute attention to the commercial side of entertainment. Art, culture, theatre (film, one might add), is a business as well as an outlet for people's ideas and feelings.

The end, once attained, is a glorious eight-minute performance of the cancan in the midst of the audience, surrounded by all of Paris, upper class and lower, at the founding of the Moulin Rouge. This great burst of energy and colour, in which everyone is caught up and which heals all jealousies, has been worth every penny and every personal betrayal. Paradoxically, although theatre it may be, it is the life-affirming energy of the final cancan that carries everything before it and sets the audience inside the film and the audience outside the film swaying and tapping to its infectious rhythms. Once again, of course, it is film that is as much on display here as theatre.

There is an edge to *French Cancan* which we should not let the conciliatory warmth of its ending obscure. Along with its apparent romantic view of the healing power of art or entertainment and the noble sacrifices of the artist, the film does not disguise something cold and unscrupulous about the emotional and financial costs involved. La Belle Abbesse, the Maria Félix character, shunts back and forth like a commodity between Danglard and Baron Walter, his financial backer. At the same time, she also knows very well how to calculate her worth as an object of (sexual) desire. By any measure, Danglard is a pimp who trades in the sexual favours of women for success in business and entertainment. He also takes advantage of the power an older man has over younger women. When Nini is first engaged, her mother automatically assumes that she is to be Danglard's mistress. In a climactic scene, Danglard explodes in anger at Nini's refusal to take the stage because he has betrayed her with his next ingénue. She only goes on when he points out that her misplaced affections for him are at the expense of her dedication to her art and to her public. La Belle Abbesse and Nini's mother both take his side. The naïveté that attends any feelings of romantic love in this environment is embodied in the pathetic figure of Prince Alexandre, a dreamy Russian prince who attempts suicide when Nini rejects him for Danglard. The future that is in store for Nini once her beauty and

BELOW
Still from 'French Cancan' (1955)
On this street set with its painted backdrop, the Reine Blanche, a Montmartre dance hall, stands where the Moulin Rouge will be built.

BOTTOM
Still from 'French Cancan' (1955)
This wonderful drawing in full colour shows a front view of what the Moulin Rouge will look like upon completion.

RIGHT
Production sketch for 'French Cancan' (1955)
The 'Reine Blanche' is in the centre background of this incredibly detailed pen and ink sketch of a period Montmartre street scene.

Still from 'French Cancan' (1955)
On stage at the opening of the Moulin Rouge, Maria Félix entertains the troops as Catherine the Great while Casimir (Phillipe Clay) looks on encouragingly.

talents have faded is represented by Prunelle. She is a beggar woman who was once a star herself but who now relies on distant memories and occasional loose change from Danglard for survival.

That sexual exploitation is a condition of Danglard's success is abundantly clear from the way in which the cancan is filmed, with its numerous tight shots of the spread thighs of the dancers and the fevered response of the male spectators. The film's honesty is such that as a frankly commercial undertaking on Renoir's part it is able to acknowledge and mediate its own apparent contradiction between a dedication to art and the demands of business, between the spectacle of the dance and the commodification of the dancers as sexual property. The cancan, *French Cancan*, cannot be realized without the admission that our delight in the dance and in the film, our delight in the dance that is the film, is at an emotional and financial cost. Given the film's period setting in Montmartre and the evocation in its colour palette and *mises en scènes* of the images of Degas, Manet, Monet, Toulouse-Lautrec and Pierre-Auguste Renoir, it also says as much about the achievement of the Impressionists, their contemporaries and their art. A lifetime of film-making and a famous father evidently taught Renoir to acquire a realistic vision of the relationship between the perfections of art or entertainment and the inevitable messiness of life.

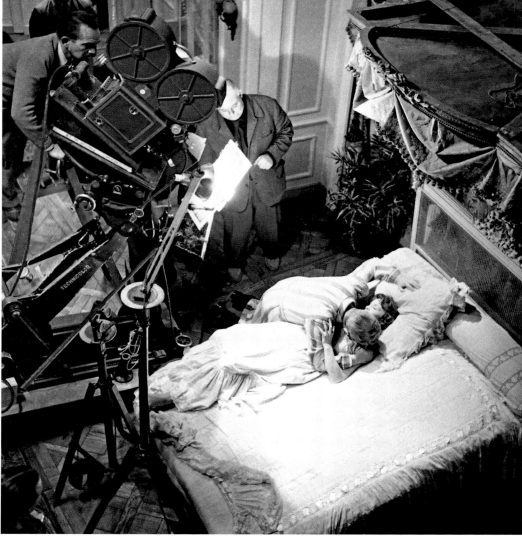

The line between honesty and cynicism is sometimes narrow, and *Elena et les hommes* (*Elena and Her Men*, 1956) is a film that may have crossed that line. Its light, tinkling surface masks an unpleasantness that is not apparent at first viewing. The period is once again the 1880s and the occasion the thinly-disguised personal and political troubles of General Georges Boulanger (General Rollan in the film). Boulanger was the hope of Royalists and Bonapartists on the French right for the restoration of France's prestige after years of ignominy following its defeat in the Franco-Prussian war of 1870-1871. On Bastille Day, 1886, after his review of the troops at Longchamps, which is where the film begins, Boulanger's popularity with the general public was at its peak. In 1889 his supporters urged him to seize political power from a weak Republican government. But Boulanger lost his nerve, rejected his chance at power, and instead ran away with his mistress. He was tried for treason in absentia, lost his mistress to illness and committed suicide on her grave.

History's story may be with Boulanger/Rollan, but the film's story is with Elena, an impoverished Polish princess, played by Ingrid Bergman in a dazzling performance. This is a film about a strong woman and three suitors, one of whom is the General, one of whom is Henri de Chevincourt, a minor aristocrat and an idler, and the third of whom is Martin-Michaud, an unattractive shoe manufacturer. *Elena and Her Men* is a woman's film because a woman tries to act as the agent of her own interests, interests that have to do both with the fulfilment of personal desire and with the exercise of power in society. Her attempt to exercise power through influence over the General is frustrated because, in a reversal of gender roles, he is more interested in her than he is in realizing any ambition to lead the country. Against the grain of romanticized womanhood, Elena intends to marry the unappealing Martin-Michaud because she has nothing left to sell except herself. (Ingrid Bergman as a prostitute!) All of her efforts to shape the future, in both the public and the private spheres, ultimately lead to the film's appropriate conclusion in a brothel, whose setting is a metaphor for how she is valued by men and for the real extent of her influence. In a complicated exchange of disguises, Henri gets Elena to admit her true love for him by impersonating the General at a brothel window in front of an adoring crowd. In this way, Elena is restored to her proper role in society as an object of desire rather than its subject. The impersonation enables the General to escape in disguise as a gypsy with his mistress to the south of France. Elena has been betrayed and political life is treated as a burlesque. The moral? "Dictatorship doesn't stand a chance in a country where affairs of the heart are so important." If the relation between political means and ends has collapsed, so has that between the private and public spheres. The only power that means anything is a function of performance, the manufacture of illusion, before an appreciative audience. That apparently includes history as a kind of performance as well as personal life.

The film's other important setting is Martin-Michaud's château, where Renoir has had the decors constructed and much of the action staged in deliberate echo of *The Rules of the Game*. The later film takes from the earlier its kitchen set shot in depth, the château's grand staircase, the pursuits upstairs and down through doors and along corridors, its character types seen hiding behind a sofa or fainting dramatically, and their disguises and mistaken identities. All contribute to the broad farce of Elena's attempt to persuade General Rollan to act. All should serve to make us aware that the film is actively reflecting upon the way it produces meaning for us and the kinds of meanings it produces. Thus, if tragedy lies beneath the farce of *The*

BELOW
Still from 'French Cancan' (1955)
La Belle Abbesse (Maria Félix) is indifferent to her suitor. She smoulders with jealousy over Danglard's infatuation with Nini.

LEFT
On the set of 'French Cancan' (1955)
With a nice attention to detail, Renoir arranges the folds of Maria Félix's dress for this scene with Jean-Roger Caussimon as Baron Walter.

PAGE 154
On the set of 'French Cancan' (1955)
The stage floor of the Francoeur Studio is lit and the dancers await their cue so that filming can begin on the cancan routine which will be the climax of the film.

PAGE 155 TOP
Still from 'French Cancan' (1955)
The brilliant colour spectacle of the cancan is in full swing amidst the patrons of the Moulin Rouge as the dancers execute a pinwheel.

PAGE 155 BOTTOM
Still from 'French Cancan' (1955)
With legs in the air and thighs exposed, this manoeuvre draws attention to the erotic power of the cancan.

153

ABOVE
Still from 'Elena et les hommes' (1956)
General Rollan (Jean Marais) attempts to make love to Elena (Ingrid Bergman) while Eugène (Jacques Jouanneau) and Lolotte (Magali Noel) look on.

RIGHT
Still from 'Elena et les hommes' (1956)
Henri (Mel Ferrer) and General Rollan prepare to duel for Elena. This and other scenes in the château intentionally echo 'The Rules of the Game'.

OPPOSITE
Publicity still for 'Elena et les hommes' (1956)
Henri and Elena pose at film's end as the film's true couple are finally united after the General has been sent on his way to the south of France with his mistress.

Rules of the Game, in disappointment that a utopian moment for change has been missed, beneath the farce of *Elena and Her Men* lies the cynicism that comes with the abandonment of political hope altogether. Renoir has come to reject the possibility of film (or art in general) contributing to social change.

After a hiatus of three and a half years, during which he staged a production of Shakespeare's *Julius Caesar (Jules César)* in the Roman arena at Arles in 1954, wrote and produced a play, *Orvet* (1955), and directed a 15-second tableau with Daniel Gélin for a Paris stage production of his own translation of Clifford Odets' *The Big Knife (Le Grand couteau)* in 1957, Renoir returned to the cinema with *Le Testament du Docteur Cordelier (The Testament of Doctor Cordelier)* and *Le Déjeuner sur l'herbe (Picnic on the Grass)* both of which were produced in 1959, although the latter was released in France first. Both were shot using similar production techniques borrowed from contemporary television practice. The action was recorded with multiple cameras simultaneously (even outdoors), so that the actors could play out their scenes with fewer interruptions for new camera set-ups. A great deal of rehearsal time was required in advance, but shooting could proceed very quickly, and the editor had the advantage of a considerable quantity and variety of footage

ABOVE
On the set of 'Elena et les hommes' (1956)
René Burri took this shot of Renoir directing Bergman and Ferrer by the open window before which they will kiss for the benefit of the crowd in the film's closing sequence.

OPPOSITE
On the set of 'Elena et les hommes' (1956)
This is another photo by Burri of the street set in front of Rosa la Rose's brothel. Renoir can be seen in conference in the centre of the street.

PAGES 158/159
On the set of 'Elena et les hommes' (1956)
Burri also took this photo of Ingrid Bergman in her riding costume at the Boulogne Studios.

Rehearsal for 'Julius Caesar' (1954)
Renoir is rehearsing his production of
Shakespeare's 'Julius Caesar' in the July heat in
the Roman arena at Arles, in the south of
France.

Performance of 'Julius Caesar' (1954)
The play is in progress on the floor of the Roman
arena at Arles on the night of 10 July 1954.
Unfortunately, no one thought to film this single
performance.

PAGES 164/165
Rehearsal for 'Orvet' (1955)
Rehearsals are in progress for Renoir's 1955 play 'Orvet'. Leslie Caron, the play's star, can be seen behind a haze of smoke at centre with her legs outstretched .

PAGES 166/167
Rehearsal for 'Orvet' (1955)
By the time he was rehearsing 'Orvet', Renoir required the actors to first read their lines like the telephone book, without intonation, and gradually build up from there.

PAGES 168/169
On the set of 'Le Grand Couteau' (1957)
Action! A 16 mm camera records the 15-second shot of Daniel Gélin slumping to the floor in Renoir's stage adaptation of Clifford Odets' 'The Big Knife' ('Le Grand Couteau').

Still from 'Le Déjeuner sur l'herbe' (1959)
Nénette (Catherine Rouvel) bathes in the river under the voyeuristic eye of Professor Alexis. Women and rivers is a motif in 'A Day in the Country', 'La Bête humaine' and 'The River'.

with which to work. Interestingly, *Picnic on the Grass* begins with a pre-credit sequence that simulates a real-time teleconference link between three different parties in prophetic anticipation of late twentieth-century electronic media practices. After the films of the early 1950s, with their historically displaced story worlds, *Picnic on the Grass* is an attempt, all but the last attempt in Renoir's career, to engage with a contemporary issue, the role of science, technology and the mass media in everyday life.

The attempt cannot be said to have been very successful, however, in so far as the film purports to be a comedy, yet is weighed down by rather simplistic oppositions between science and nature, technology and passion. The contrast lacks tension and subtlety, so that the strokes that paint each position are far too broad (and, frankly, humourless). The heavy-handedness is redeemed somewhat by the extraordinary beauty of Catherine Rouvel in the role of Nénette, and the cinematography which takes advantage of the film's primary location on the grounds of Les Collettes, the former Renoir family property at Cagnes-sur-mer. This is where Pierre-Auguste painted many of his late works, such as the magnificent canvases in his series of bathers. Jean, of course, spent parts of many years of his boyhood, adolescence and young manhood here. This is where he met Catherine Hessling, the painter's model who became his first wife. The film's setting amongst

'Oh, Freud, what crimes have been committed in thy name!'

Jean Renoir

ABOVE
Still from 'Le Déjeuner sur l'herbe' (1959)
Everyone gets ready to settle down for the night around the campfire. Professor Alexis (Paul Meurisse) holds Nénette in his arms.

TOP LEFT
On the set of 'Le Déjeuner sur l'herbe' (1959)
Renoir sets up a group shot of the campers. Paulette Dubost, who played Lisette in 'The Rules of the Game' in 1939, is in the centre with the frying pan.

LEFT
On the set of 'Le Déjeuner sur l'herbe' (1959)
François Truffaut, who is about to make his own first film, 'The 400 Blows', visits his idol on location.

171

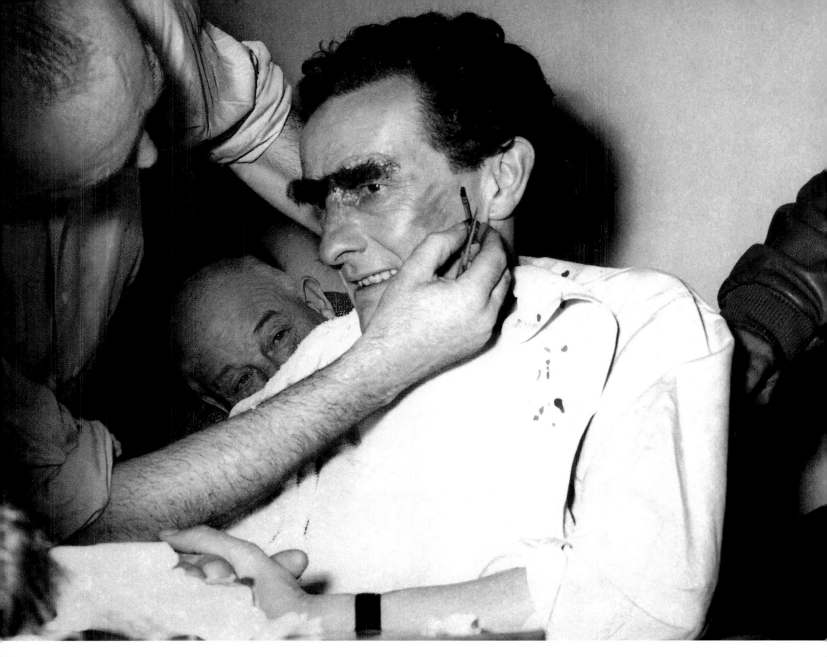

the olive trees, the fields, the flowers and the coach house on this property lend it an unmistakeable autobiographical dimension. Its title *Picnic on the Grass* evokes a world and a practice of art that we and Renoir may be inclined to romanticize as anti-technological, an illusion that the film certainly does nothing to dispel. During this period in the late 1950s, Renoir was also working on *Renoir, My Father*, the superb biography of Pierre-Auguste, which appeared in 1962. There he frequently takes the occasion to attribute to his father various jeremiads against blind progress and the fetishization of technology.

The world of modern science is represented in the film by Etienne Alexis, a proponent of artificial insemination (if not quite eugenics). He regards passion as a vestigial characteristic of human beings of which they should be cured like the common cold (for which, as we all know, there is no cure!). He is to be married to Marie-Charlotte, a health fanatic, and the stern head of the European girl scout movement. He is French, she German, and their spiritless marriage will herald the formation of a new European union dedicated to rational principles about human perfectibility. However, even science and rationality are subject to the effects of the *mistral*, a feverish wind generated by the pan pipe of Gaspard, a Dionysian figure who is associated with a pet goat and a ruined temple of Diana. The wind arouses people's instincts, excites their appetites (for sex, for food) and sends Etienne Alexis into the arms of the beautiful Nénette, the daughter of a well-fed, indulgent Provençal father. Alexis foregoes science, rationality and artificial insemination, in favour of instinct, passion and sex after he sees Nénette bathing nude in the river. Shots of nature's flow, the wind in the trees, water in the river, colourful grasses that bend to both wind and water, are symptomatic of a turbulence within and without that leads Alexis to the conclusion that "perhaps happiness is a submission to the natural order." Alexis comes to his senses (so to speak) when he rejects Marie-Charlotte in favour of Nénette, who is pregnant with the child they have produced while lying in one another's arms. The marriage of science with nature is the future of the new Europe.

Renoir's work is not noted for its use of the figure of the doppelgänger or double, perhaps because, for the most part, he eschewed any psychological interests. That makes *The Testament of Doctor Cordelier* all the more surprising, since it is a free adaptation of Robert Louis Stevenson's *Dr. Jekyll and Mr. Hyde*. The film is set in a contemporary, modernist, functional Paris and one of its mysterious, decaying suburbs. It opens with a sequence in a television studio in which Renoir appears as himself to introduce his film as though it were a document reporting on a psychological and social reality. Stylistically, the crisp, high-contrast black-and-white cinematography perfectly suits a theme dear to the tradition of film noir. An alternative title for the Renoir film in English is *Experiment in Evil*, which explains something of its narrative impulse. Dr. Cordelier is a psychiatrist who has led an ambivalent existence. He is both guilt-ridden at having had affairs with his patients, and ascetic in limiting most human contacts. Self-disgust at his own base instincts is a powerful motive when Cordelier decides to embark on a study of the origins of his and our evil impulses. Cordelier therefore experiments with a potion that will cure him of moral corruption. Instead, the potion transforms him into a creature free of all constraint, without conscience, the purely anti-social Opale. When the Doctor releases the Opale inside him, this terrible figure wanders the streets terrorizing, maiming, or killing children, mothers with babies, the disabled, women, and the elderly. In short, with one exception, he visits his cruelties primarily upon those who

'…*there are no white horses, any more than there are black horses. There are dark grey horses, light grey horses, dark chestnut horses, and light bay horses; in short, there isn't a single horse that doesn't have a few hairs of another colour. Clichés do not exist in nature or in life. So there shouldn't be any in my films.*'

Jean Renoir

ABOVE
Still from 'Le Testament du Docteur Cordelier' (1959)
In a scene that underlines Opale's wanton cruelty, he sweeps the crutches out from under a disabled passerby and sends him crashing to the pavement.

OPPOSITE TOP
On the set of 'Le Testament du Docteur Cordelier' (1959)
A fastidious and time-consuming make-up job was required to turn Jean-Louis Barrault's Dr. Cordelier into Opale, his evil alter ego.

OPPOSITE BOTTOM
Rehearsals for 'Le Testament du Docteur Cordelier' (1959)
A lot of time was spent in rehearsal before any decisions were made about camera setups. This scene did not make into the film.

Still from 'Le Caporal épinglé' (1962)
The Corporal (Jean-Pierre Cassel) and Papa
(Claude Brasseur) are foiled in their first attempt
at escape under cover of darkness.

are society's most vulnerable. The exception is his murder of a fellow psychiatrist and rival, the wildly neurotic Dr. Séverin, who thinks Cordelier's experiments on the sources of evil are mad. These targets of Opale's irrational behaviour make his nature seem all the more pointlessly evil. An especially remarkable and disturbing scene (because it shakes the spectator's complacencies) is that in which Opale kicks away the double crutches supporting a disabled passer-by to bring him crashing painfully to the sidewalk. Part of the point, one supposes, is that there is an Opale inside all of us, barely constrained by the conventions of society and the thin veneer of our 'civilisation.'

Most of the film's energy comes from the performance of Jean-Louis Barrault as both the distinguished, white-haired Dr. Cordelier and as his manic alter ego, Opale. On screen as Opale, Barrault is riveting and his transformation a wonder. Against Cordelier's dignity of appearance and calm, there is Opale's frenetic energy. His clothes are too big, ill-fitting, and constantly dishevelled. He walks in a bouncing, rolling gait, twitching his limbs and body and with his head thrust forward. His hands and arms are excessively hairy, his face misshapen, and one shoulder is higher than the other. While Opale's acts make him a demon, a monster, there is

Still from 'Le Caporal épinglé' (1962)
In yet another unsuccessful attempt at escape
from a work camp, the Corporal and Papa are
dumped unceremoniously from the back of a
truck carrying bricks.

nevertheless something compelling for the spectator about his presence by virtue of
the skill of Barrault's performance. One has difficulty believing this is the same actor
in the roles of both Cordelier and Opale, so convincing is the transformation.

Over the remainder of the 1960s, Renoir would direct two more films, write
another play, *Carola*, broadcast on U.S. television in 1973, publish a very good
novel, *Les Cahiers du Capitaine Georges* (*The Notebooks of Captain Georges*) in
1966, and participate in a documentary about his method of rehearsing actors, *La
Direction d'acteurs par Jean Renoir* in 1970. The praise heaped on Renoir by Truffaut,
Godard, Rivette, Rohmer and company in the 1950s and 1960s and their keen
interest in his past and present work may have been an encouragement to Renoir to
go on making films despite his advancing age. Like *Grand Illusion*, the action of *Le
Caporal épinglé* (*The Elusive Corporal*, 1962) is built around various escape attempts
by French soldiers from German prison camps, this time with a Second World War
setting. *The Elusive Corporal* borrows something from New Wave innovations in its
use of interpolated newsreel footage to present some of the major military
engagements of the war, especially as those determined the fate of France. The
fictional story world of the film, then, has to be seen as Renoir's response to the fall

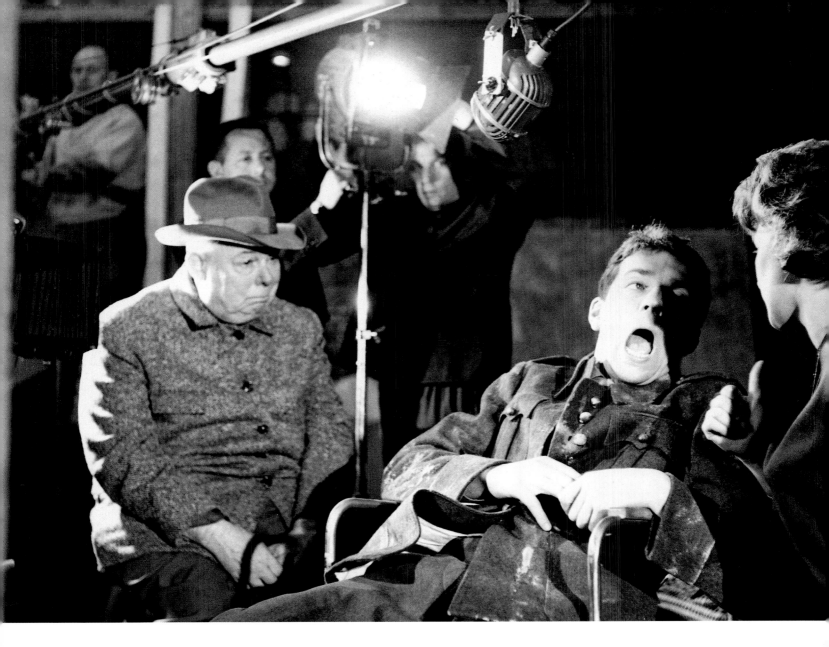

On the set of 'Le Caporal épinglé' (1962)
Renoir seems in sympathy with Jean-Pierre
Cassel's cry of pain as he directs this scene in
the dentist's office with Cornelia Froboess as
Erika.

of France and the German Occupation. Under the terms of the armistice, the
soldiers in the film are prisoners of war and subjected to forced labour. They exist in
a kind of limbo between commitment and withdrawal. They are soldiers still, but in
a situation of bad faith. Their various escape attempts can be regarded as attempts to
resolve the issue of their responsibility, a resolution that cannot be achieved on the
part of the eponymous Corporal of the title (i.e. he is every corporal) until he passes
through a series of trials that involve failed escape attempts as well as the sacrifices
of others. He has to understand why he needs to escape if his escape is to be
meaningful.

Two important characters who abet his escape are Ballochet, a close friend, and
Erika, a German dental assistant. The first offers him moral guidance and the second
material assistance. Ballochet has given in to bad faith by accepting the creature
comforts that come with abandoning all resistance to his German captors. In the
ivory tower of his pride inside the prison, he insists that he is more free than he was
on the outside, in Paris, before the war, where he was a slave to habit and
convention. By correcting Erika's French and reading Ronsard to her, the Corporal is
lead to dream of the civilian life outside, and strengthens his resolve not to be a slave
to the Germans or the routine of prison camp life. When he takes this lesson back to

ABOVE
On the set of 'Le Caporal épinglé' (1962)
Renoir directs the film's penultimate sequence
as the Corporal listens to the helpful French
farmer who is content to stay where he is with his
German wife.

LEFT
On the set of 'Le Caporal épinglé' (1962)
A little horseplay on the set, as Renoir and
Cassell make fun of the actor who is being made
up to play the part of the 'female' escapee on the
train.

Banochet, the latter confesses to his bad faith, and elects to seek his freedom through an 'escape' into assisted suicide by the German guards. With Erika's help, the Corporal and Papa, another prisoner, manage to make it onto a train. The train is bombed in a *Götterdämmerung* of fire and smoke just as a drunken (German) passenger shouts "Vive la France!" When the two French escapees make it to Paris and the Pont de Tolbiac, the Corporal says two things in parting. The first is that Paris is beautiful and that one can breathe its air, despite the smell of gasoline. The second is that he finds swastikas depressing. The connection could not be clearer. In a conclusion that seems very different to any of Renoir's other post-war films, acquiescence is no answer to the problem of freedom and its accompanying responsibility. Only an act in good faith will answer to the existential dilemma posed by the condition of one's being in the world.

With *The Little Theatre of Jean Renoir* (1969) our long conversation with Jean Renoir comes to a close, at least through the medium of film. Anyone who so wishes can continue this conversation through his autobiography, *Ma Vie et mes films* (*My Life and My Films*, 1974), and through the three novels that Renoir wrote in his last years, *Le Coeur à l'aise* (1978), *Le Crime de l'anglais* (1979), and *Geneviève* (1979). The autobiography and the novels are simply another medium for many of the subjects that have preoccupied Renoir in the course of a long life. Renoir's last film stands up better with the passage of time than might have been expected. The themes, the styles and the structure of *The Little Theatre of Jean Renoir* all lead one to believe that Renoir was well aware that this was to be his last film. Of course, the title itself sounds like a summary testament to a whole career. The film is organized as four independent, fictional sketches, each with its own cast of characters and each with its own style. Each sketch is introduced by Renoir, and each seems to engage with a theme that belongs to one of the four major periods of his career: the inequities of social class; the horrors of technology; the fleetingness of passion; the futility of struggle. The opening shot of the film introduces the tension between theatre and life, reality and artifice, that we know he knows informs so many of his films individually and so much of his work as a whole. An old, stooped Jean Renoir, looking every bit his 75 years of age (in 1969), stands beside a little model stage which serves as a prop with which to introduce the first sketch.

'Le Dernier Réveillon' ('The Last Christmas Eve'), the first sketch, takes us back to the fantasy world of Hans Christian Andersen (to whom the sketch is dedicated) and Renoir's *The Little Match Girl*. A tramp is paid by a jaded diner to stand at a restaurant window and look in on a table of customers gorging themselves on a festive dinner of caviar, turkey, pâté de foie gras and champagne. Although his motives are suspect, by exposing the contrast between rich and poor, warmth and cold, plenty and poverty, the cynical diner succeeds in proving that "Christmas is the greatest cliché of our civilisation". The other customers get up and leave in discomfort at having the tables turned (so to speak) by being made a spectacle (for once) instead of spectators. The tramp is given the leftovers. He and his female companion create their own Christmas fantasy under a bridge by the Seine, where they waltz to imaginary music in an imaginary château until they succumb to the bitter cold. While the satire is bitter, unfortunately the solace that the tramps find in each other in death makes for a rather saccharine conclusion.

'La Cireuse électrique' ('The Electric Floor Polisher'), the second sketch, which Renoir described as an 'opera', is a modern, urban story set in a generic, one bedroom apartment amidst a new high-rise complex. Such sterile, cookie-cutter

On the set of 'Le Petit théâtre de Jean Renoir' (1969)
Top: The camera is set up under the bridge set with a painted Paris spread out in the background ready to film the two tramps of 'Le Dernier Réveillon'.
Bottom: Renoir directs the two tramps played by Nino Formicola and Milly Monti, champagne glasses in hand, for the scene of their Christmas dinner under the bridge.

TOP
Still from 'Le Petit théâtre de Jean Renoir' (1969)
In 'La Cireuse électrique', the first husband (Pierre Olaf) slips on the newly polished parquet floor and cracks his head open.

ABOVE
Still from 'Le Petit théâtre de Jean Renoir' (1969)
The second husband commits the unpardonable atrocity of sending the polisher plunging to its death from the balcony of the highrise apartment.

building forms were thrown up around the perimeter of Paris in the 1960s to house the clerks and petty functionaries of a new generation of post-war consumers. The film's theme is man and the machine. A housewife, Emilie, is obsessed with waxing her parquet floor. She persuades her husband, Gustave, to buy her an electric floor polisher on pain of leaving him. He promptly slips on a newly polished patch of floor and cracks his head open. Her love affair with the machine is a fetishistic substitute for her relationship with her husband. One day her new husband, Jules, has had enough and reclaims his authority and his masculinity by throwing the polisher off the balcony to its death on the street below. Emilie commits suicide for love by following the polisher out the window. This domestic melodrama is accompanied by a chorus of office workers who sing that to cause the death of a human being is bad enough, but to murder a machine is an abomination. Stylistically, this sketch combines a realism of milieu with the performance of song and mime. There is a very clever use of an animated black-and-white photograph of the deceased first husband in dumb-show conversation with the beleaguered second. Thematically, the film is a satire of our seduction by technology in modernity, a theme that was always close to Renoir, but which only came to full flower (so to speak) with *Picnic on the Grass*. Perhaps Renoir's experience of America's love affair with technology and its influence on France's 30-year period of prosperity after World War Two (the *trentes glorieuses*) found its way into the theme of this sketch. However, because the humour is not always sharp, the satire is a little weak.

The third sketch, entitled 'Quand l'amour meurt' ('When Love Dies'), is very interesting. It consists in its entirety of three shots of Jeanne Moreau dressed in period costume of the Belle Epoque (a beautiful off-the-shoulder, yellow and black, full-length evening dress) standing on a stage against a painted backdrop of a nature scene while mournfully singing the title song. Moreau contributes to the haunting quality of the performance by a curious tilt of her head to one side while she sings. The first shot and the last are long shots, the second a close shot in which the camera first moves slowly forward to a full close-up, and then retreats as slowly to a medium shot, thereby emphasizing her isolation and lending an extraordinary pathos to the meaning of her (love) song. This is not a song of nostalgia, but a song of loss, of lost love, lost time, of a history lost.

The last of the four sketches in Renoir's *Little Theatre* is 'Le Roi d'Yvetot' ('The King of Yvetot'). This is vintage Renoir and a fitting close to his film career. Of the four sketches, it depends most on the conventions of realism familiar to us from his work during the 1930s. Further, there are uniformly excellent performances from all of the principals (two of whom, Andrex and Ardisson, had appeared all those years ago in *Toni* and *La Marseillaise*, respectively), including Françoise Arnoul, Fernand Sardou, Jean Carmet and Dominique Labourier, a giddy newcomer with an infectious laugh. True to his adage that 'one starts with the environment to arrive at the self', Renoir sets his story of cuckoldry and gossip on location in the south of France. The film arrives at collective laughter as the solution to the pettiness of individual jealousy and private rancour. Isabelle, a beautiful, somewhat restless woman in early middle age, is married to Edmond, a considerably older man. He is content to play *boules* or cards in the village square and is a little uneasy that his wife might be unhappy. M. Féraud, the local doctor, is called to the house on an emergency and somewhat innocently begins a passionate affair with Isabelle. They ease their consciences in the knowledge that Edmond is happy because Isabelle is happy, although Edmond is ignorant of the affair until the day he faces a closed door

On the set of 'Le Petit théâtre de Jean Renoir' (1969)
Renoir with Jeanne Moreau, who is dressed in the splendid gown she wears to perform the song 'Quand l'amour meurt'.

that hides an unwelcome truth. At the film's conclusion, during a game of *boules* in the public square, private lives are laid bare before the whole community, but all is forgiven everyone, and the entire cast turns and bows theatrically to the camera on behalf of themselves and of Renoir, as though in acknowledgement of his entire *oeuvre*. We can return the acknowledgement by applauding such an intelligent, thoroughly enjoyable, life-long conversation with one of the world's great film-makers.

ABOVE
Stills from 'Le Petit théâtre de Jean Renoir' (1969)
Duvallier (Fernand Sardou) lines up a throw at a game of boules in the village square. Too much attention to boules threatens to lose him a wife.

PAGES 182/183
Jean Renoir
Douglas Kirkland took this photo of Jean in his Beverly Hills home in conversation with students. Pierre-Auguste's bust of Jean's mother stands behind him; 'Le Chasseur' is on the wall in front of him.

'I have spent my life experimenting with different styles, but it all comes down to this: my different attempts to arrive at the inward truth, which for me is the only one that matters.'

Jean Renoir

Chronology

BELOW
Jean Renoir at Le Cannet (1902)

RIGHT
Jean Renoir in 'La P'tite Lili' (1927)
Evidently, Renoir enjoyed hamming it up for his part in Aberto Cavalcanti's short film.

FAR RIGHT
Jean Renoir and his son Alain during shooting of 'La Règle du jeu' (1939)
This was taken on the corridor set for the film. Alain is a very handsome 18-year-old. He worked on the film as an assistant cameraman.

1894 Born 15 September in Montmartre to Pierre-Auguste Renoir and Aline Charigot. Grows up in a house filled with women and is especially close to his nurse Gabrielle Renard, his mother's cousin from Burgundy. She introduces him to the cinema for the first time at the Dufayel department store.

1901 Birth of his younger brother, Claude ("Coco"). His older brother, Pierre, was born in 1885 and became one of the great French actors of the first half of the 20th century.

1913 Passes his baccalaureat in philosophy. Birth of his nephew, Claude, son of Pierre, who will become his cameraman in the 1930s.

1914–1918 Serves in World War One, first with the Chasseurs Alpins and then with the French Flying Corps assigned to aerial reconnaissance, where he learns both to take photographs and to fly a plane.

1915 Severely wounded in his right leg and left with a pronounced limp that will stay with him the rest of his life. Death of Jean's mother.

1916 While on military leave discovers the films of Charlie Chaplin and becomes a dedicated cinéphile.

1919 Death of Pierre-Auguste Renoir at Cagnes-sur-mer.

1920 Marries Andrée Heuschling, one of his father's last models. Jean and Andrée become devotees of cinema and adore the work of D.W. Griffith and Erich von Stroheim.

1920–1923 With his wife and various friends, including Paul Cézanne, Jr., Renoir works as a potter and ceramist.

1921 Birth of Renoir's son, Alain.

1924 Makes his first film, *Catherine*, starring his wife, who changes her name to Catherine Hessling.

1931 Breaks with Catherine Hessling prior to the shooting of *La Chienne*, his first major sound film.

1931–1939 Companion of Marguerite Houllé, his film editor throughout this period.

1935 With the participation of Jacques Prévert and the October Group, shoots the anarcho-syndicalist *Le Crime de Monsieur Lange*.

1936 *Les Bas-Fonds* wins the Prix Louis Delluc as the best French film of the year.

1935–1939 Contributes numerous articles on cinema to various, mostly left-wing, publications.

1936 Becomes allied with the French Communist Party, helps to found Ciné-liberté, a Party film production and education unit, and makes *La Vie est à nous* under the Party's auspices for the June election campaign.

1937 *La Grande Illusion* is released to great acclaim in France and achieves international success, including a special International Jury Cup at the Venice Biennale. Renoir is made a Chevalier of the Legion of Honour.

1937–1938 Writes sixty weekly feature columns for *Ce Soir*, a French Communist Party newspaper.

1938 Achieves another national and international success with *La Bête humaine*. *La Grande Illusion* opens a 26-week engagement in New York and is voted best foreign film of the year by the National Board of Review.

1939 *La Règle du jeu* is released in the summer to a mixed response. Renoir breaks with Marguerite and leaves for Italy with Dido Freire to shoot an adaptation of *La Tosca*.

1940 With the fall of France Renoir and Dido make their way to the family home in Cagnes-sur-mer. Eventually they get to Lisbon where they take passage for the United States and arrive on the last day of the year.

1941 Signs with 20th Century-Fox for whom he makes *Swamp Water*.

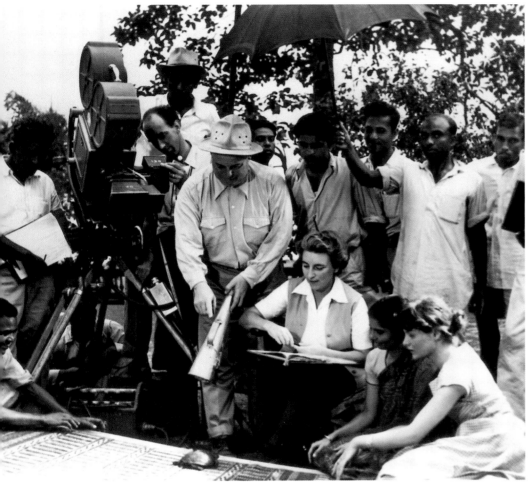

1942 Discouraged by his experience with Fox, Renoir signs with Universal, only to withdraw from a Deanna Durbin film.

1941–1949 Active on behalf of an American Popular Front with various cultural and quasi-political organisations.

1942–1943 Makes *This Land is Mine* in response to the German Occupation of France.

1944 Marries Dido Freire in Hollywood.

1945 *The Southerner*, his most successful American film, is released to critical and popular acclaim.

1946 *The Southerner* receives a best film award at the Venice Biennale. Renoir becomes a naturalized United States citizen.

1949–1950 Possibly "graylisted" from ever working in Hollywood again, Renoir elects to go to India and make *The River*, an experience that changes his life.

1951 Renoir and Dido make their formal return to France. At the Venice Biennale, *The River* shares the International Critics Prize.

1952 The first special issue of a new French film magazine, *Cahiers du cinéma*, is entirely devoted to his work. Throughout the 1950s and early 1960s, *Cahiers* champions Renoir, interviews him at length, and esteems him as the father of the New Wave.

1952–1953 Makes *The Golden Coach* in Italy, his first European film in more than a dozen years.

1954 Returns to filmmaking in France with *French Cancan*, a popular and critical success.

1958 At the Brussels World's Fair, *La Grande Illusion* is voted one of the 12 greatest films ever made.

1959 *La Règle du jeu* is reconstructed to huge acclaim in a version that runs 106 minutes.

1960 Appointed Regents' Professor of English and Dramatic Art, University of California, Berkeley.

1962 Publishes a biography of his father. A *Sight and Sound* poll votes *La Règle du jeu* one of the three greatest films of all time, a distinction which it will hold for the next 40 years.

1966 Publishes his first novel, *Les Cahiers du Capitaine Georges*.

1969 Makes *Le Petit théâtre de Jean Renoir*, his last film.

1974 Publication of his autobiography, *Ma Vie et mes films* (*My Life and My Films*) and his collected writings, *Ecrits 1926-1971* (ed. Claude Gauteur).

1979 Dies 12 February in Beverly Hills. Interred in Essoyes, Burgundy.

Filmography

LE COMPTOIR FRANÇAIS CINÉMATOGRAPHIQUE PRÉSENTE :

la nuit du carrefour

AVEC
PIERRE RENOIR
et
WINNA WINFRIED
d'après le roman de GEORGES SIMENON
adaptation et mise en scène de Jean Renoir
PRODUCTION EUROPA FILMS

Nana *(1926)*

Crew: *Director & Producer* Jean Renoir, *Scenario & Adaptation* Pierre Lestringuez, B&W, silent, 105 minutes.

Cast: Catherine Hessling (Nana), Werner Krauss (Muffat), Jean Angelo (Vandeuvres), Raymond Guérin-Catelain (Georges).

Nana, a vulgar stage performer, becomes a courtesan to Parisian high society and accumulates enormous wealth. Her insatiable appetite and complete lack of conscience drive men to suicide. As a symbol and effect of her corruption, she dies of smallpox.

Sur un air de Charleston
(Charleston, 1927)

Crew: *Director & Producer* Jean Renoir, *Scenario* Pierre Lestringuez, B&W, silent, 17 minutes.

Cast: Catherine Hessling (the dancer), Johnny Hudgins (the explorer).

A black African explorer arrives by spaceship in a post-apocalyptic Paris where he is taught the Charleston by a native white savage.

Marquitta *(1927)*

Crew: *Director* Jean Renoir, *Producer* M. Gargour, *Scenario* Pierre Lestringuez, B&W, silent, 120 minutes.

Cast: Marie-Louise Iribe (Marquitta), Jean Angelo (Prince Vlasco), Henri Debain (Count Dimitrieff, his Chamberlain).

Marquitta is a poor street-singer with whom Prince Vlasco falls in love, but then disowns when he suspects her of stealing a jewel. Their fortunes are then reversed; she becomes famous and he poor. Reconciliation is achieved after a car chase on the Riviera.

Catherine
(Une vie sans joie, 1924/1927)

Crew: *Directors* Albert Dieudonné, Jean Renoir, *Producer* Jean Renoir, *Scenario* Jean Renoir, Pierre Lestringuez, B&W, silent, 55 minutes.

Cast: Catherine Hessling (Catherine Ferrand), Louis Gauthier (Georges Mallet), Maud Richard (Edith Mallet), Jean Renoir (the sub-prefect), Albert Dieudonné (Maurice Laisné, the nephew).

After being cast out of the community by the hypocritical bourgeoisie of a small provincial town, Catherine, a poor kitchen-maid, almost plunges to her death on a runaway tram but is rescued by Georges Mallet.

La Fille de l'eau
(The Whirlpool of Fate, 1924)

Crew: *Director & Producer* Jean Renoir, *Scenario* Pierre Lestringuez, B&W, silent, 58 minutes.

Cast: Catherine Hessling (Virginie), Pierre Lestringuez (Uncle Jeff), Pierre Champagne (Justin Crépoix), Harold Livingston (Georges Raynal), Maurice Touzé (the Ferret).

Virginie is tormented by her predatory Uncle Jeff. In flight from his advances, she is first taken in by "the Ferret", a poacher, and becomes a creature of the woods. After a night of terrible dreams, she is rescued by the kind-hearted Georges, who also settles scores with Uncle Jeff.

UN FILM DE JEAN RENOIR
UNE PARTIE
DE CAMPAGNE
D'APRES GUY DE MAUPASSANT
SYLVIA BATAILLE
GEORGES D'ARNOUX · JEANNE MARKEN · JACQUES BOREL · PAUL TEMPS · GABRIELLE FONTAN
GABRIELLO

La Petite marchande d'allumettes
(The Little Match Girl, 1928)
Crew: *Directors & Producers* Jean Renoir, Jean Tedesco, *Scenario & Adaptation* Jean Renoir, B&W, silent, 29 minutes.
Cast: Catherine Hessling (the match girl), Jean Storm (the young man Axel, the soldier), Manuel Raaby (the policeman, Death).
This film adapts Hans Christian Andersen's story of the impoverished match seller whose wish-fulfilling fantasy brings to life the magic world of a toyshop as she lies dying in the snow from cold and hunger.

Tire-au-flanc *(1928)*
Crew: *Director* Jean Renoir, *Producer* Pierre Braunberger, *Scenario & Adaptation* Jean Renoir, Claude Heymann, B&W, silent, 82 minutes.
Cast: Georges Pomiès (Jean), Michel Simon (Joseph), Jeanne Helbling (Solange), Fridette Fatton (Georgette), Zellas (Muflot), Kinny Dorlay (Lily).
In this military farce, Jean, a poet, and Joseph, his servant, are called up for military service. The impractical Jean is bullied by Muflot, a fellow soldier, until he turns the tables at the Colonel's fête. The happy outcome is the union of three couples: Joseph with Georgette, Lt. Daumel with Solange, and Jean with Lily.

Le Tournoi *(1929)*
Crew: *Director* Jean Renoir, *Producer* Henri Dupuy-Mazuel, *Scenario* Henri Dupuy-Mazuel, André Jaeger-Schmidt, B&W, silent, 106 minutes.
Cast: Aldo Nadi (François de Baynes), Suzanne Desprès (Countess de Baynes), Jackie Monnier (Isabelle Ginori), Manuel Raaby (Count Ginori), Enrique Rivero (Henri de Rogier).
A film commissioned to mark the 2000th anniversary of the founding of the city of Carcassonne, it showcases the city and its famous walls using an historical costume drama involving Catholic and Protestant enmities set at the French court of Catherine de' Medicis.

Le Bled *(1929)*
Crew: *Director* Jean Renoir, *Producer* Henri Dupuy-Mazuel, *Scenario* Henri Dupuy-Mazuel, André Jaeger-Schmidt, B&W, silent, 96 minutes.
Cast: Alexandre Arquillère (Christian Hoffer), Enrique Rivero (Pierre Hoffer), Jackie Monnier (Claudie Duvernet), Manuel Raaby (Manuel Duvernet), Diana Hart (Diane Duvernet).
An interesting propaganda film on behalf of the French in Algeria which exoticizes the attractions of the landscape and the customs of the inhabitants while developing a fictional intrigue about a contested inheritance.

On purge bébé *(1931)*
Crew: *Director* Jean Renoir, *Producer* Charles David, *Scenario & Adaptation* Jean Renoir, Pierre Prévert, B&W, 46 minutes.
Cast: Jacques Louvigny (Fallavoine), Marguerite Pierry (Julie Fallavoine), Sacha Tarride (Toto), Michel Simon (Chouilloux), Fernandel (Truchet).
M. Chouilloux arrives at the Fallavoine household to listen to a pitch about buying chamber pots for the French army. Toto is constipated. Chouilloux believes himself cuckolded. The latter drinks the purgative intended for the former. Toto is relieved.

La Chienne *(The Bitch, 1931)*
Crew: *Director & Scenario & Adaptation* Jean Renoir, *Producer* Charles David, B&W, 94 minutes.
Cast: Michel Simon (Maurice Legrand), Janie Marèse (Lulu), Georges Flamant (Dédé), Magdeleine Berubet (Adèle Legrand).
Naïve M. Legrand falls for Lulu, a prostitute, whom he sets up in her own apartment. She and her pimp, Dédé, gull him into passing over his Sunday paintings which they sell on the art market. When the scales drop from his eyes, he murders Lulu and Dédé is executed for the crime.

La Nuit du Carrefour
(Night at the Crossroads, 1932)
Crew: *Director & Scenario & Adaptation* Jean Renoir, *Producer* Jacques Becker, B&W, 74 minutes.
Cast: Pierre Renoir (Inspector Maigret), Winna Winfried (Else Andersen), Georges Koudria (Carl Andersen), Georges Térof (Lucas).
In the course of investigating a murder, Inspector Maigret puts an end to a ring of smugglers operating out of an isolated crossroads in the countryside south of Paris.

Boudu sauvé des eaux
(Boudu Saved From Drowning, 1932)
Crew: *Director* Jean Renoir, *Producers* Pierre Braunberger, Roger Richebé, *Scenario & Adaptation* Jean Renoir, Albert Valentin, B&W, 84 minutes.
Cast: Michel Simon (Boudu), Charles Granval (Edouard Lestingois), Marcelle Hainia (Emma Lestingois), Séverine Lerczinska (Anne-Marie).
Boudu, a distraught tramp, throws himself into the Seine, is rescued by a well-meaning bookseller and brought into his home. Boudu creates havoc in this respectable bourgeois world until he is returned at film's end to the milieu from which he came.

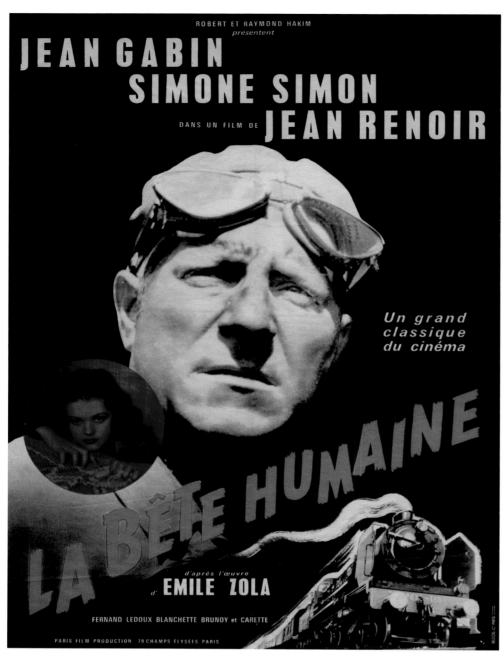

ROBERT ET RAYMOND HAKIM
présentent

JEAN GABIN
SIMONE SIMON
DANS UN FILM DE **JEAN RENOIR**

Un grand classique du cinéma

LA BÊTE HUMAINE

d'après l'œuvre d' **EMILE ZOLA**

FERNAND LEDOUX BLANCHETTE BRUNOY et CARETTE

PARIS FILM PRODUCTION 79 CHAMPS ÉLYSÉES PARIS

---

takes responsibility for the murder on her behalf and is shot and killed by the authorities.

Le Crime de Monsieur Lange
(The Crime of Mr. Lange, 1936)
Crew: *Director* Jean Renoir, *Producer* Geneviève Blondeau, *Scenario* Jean Renoir, Jacques Prévet, B&W, 84 minutes.
Cast: René Lefèvre (Amédée Lange), Jules Berry (Batala), Florelle (Valentine), Nadia Sibirskaïa (Estelle), Sylvia Bataille (Edith).
When Batala, the exploitative owner of a publishing firm, dies in a train wreck, the employees form a cooperative and publish the stories of M. Lange. Unexpectedly, Batala returns, but is killed by Lange so that the co-op can continue. Lange flees the country with Valentine.

La Vie est à nous *(Life Is Ours, 1936)*
Crew: *Directors* Jean Renoir, Jean-Paul Le Chanois, Jacques Becker, Pierre Unik, Henri Cartier-Bresson, André Zwobada, Marc Maurette, Jacques Brunius, *Scenario* Jean Renoir, Jean-Paul Le Chanois, Pierre Unik, B&W, 62 minutes.
Cast: Jean Dasté (the teacher), Charles Blavette (a metal worker), Max Dalban (the foreman), Eddy Debray (the auctioneer), Gaston Modot (the farmer's nephew), Léon Larive (a potential bidder), Julien Bertheau (René), Nadia Sibirskaïa (Ninette).
A didactic film comprising both documentary and fictional episodes made and performed by a collective on behalf of the Parti Communiste Français for the 1936 French elections.

Partie de campagne
(A Day in the Country, 1936)
Crew: *Director & Scenario & Adaptation* Jean Renoir, Producer Pierre Braunberger, B&W, 40 minutes.

Paulette **GODDARD**
BURGESS MEREDITH
HURD HATFIELD
FRANCIS LEDERER

MEMORIAS *de una* **DONCELLA**

Chotard & Cie. *(1933)*
Crew: *Director* Jean Renoir, *Producer & Scenario & Adaptation* Roger Ferdinand, B&W, 83 minutes.
Cast: Fernand Charpin (François Chotard), Georges Pomiès (Julien Collinet), Reine Chotard (Jeanne Boitel).
M. Chotard is a success in the retail food business and a stalwart of his community. However, his daughter falls in love with a scatter-brained poet, Julien Collinet, who is only reconciled to his father-in-law when he wins the Prix Goncourt.

Madame Bovary *(1934)*
Crew: *Director & Scenario & Adaptation* Jean Renoir, *Producer* Gaston Gallimard, B&W, 102 minutes.
Cast: Valentine Tessier (Emma Bovary), Pierre Renoir (Charles Bovary), Fernand Fabre (Rodolphe), Daniel Lecourtois (Léon), Max Dearly (Homais), Robert Le Vigan (Lheureux).
In the provinces near Rouen, Emma marries Charles Bovary, the local doctor, but takes up with a succession of lovers to escape her stifling environment. When her excessive debts are about to be revealed to her stolid husband, she commits suicide by poisoning.

Toni *(1935)*
Crew: *Director* Jean Renoir, *Producer* Pierre Gaut, *Scenario* Jean Renoir, Carl Einstein, B&W, 84 minutes.
Cast: Charles Blavette (Toni), Celia Montalvan (Joséfa), Jenny Hélia (Marie), Max Dalban (Albert), Andrex (Gabi).
Toni goes to the south of France to find work and falls in love with Joséfa. She is forced to marry Albert, who abuses her until she kills him. Toni

Cast: Sylvia Bataille (Henriette), Georges Darnoux (Henri), Jeanne Marken (Mme. Dufour), Jacques Brunius (Rodolphe).

In the course of a Sunday excursion to the country from Paris with her petit-bourgeois family, Henriette has her first sexual experience with Henri. Years later, married to an oaf, she returns to the scene of her seduction and meets Henri once again.

Les Bas-Fonds *(The Lower Depths, 1936)*
Crew: *Director* Jean Renoir, *Producer* Alexander Kamenka, *Scenario* Jean Renoir, Charles Spaak, B&W, 92 minutes.
Cast: Jean Gabin (Pépel), Louis Jouvet (the Baron), Vladimir Sokoloff (Kostylev), Junie Astor (Natacha), Suzy Prim (Vassilissa).
A discredited Baron meets an inveterate thief and both end up in the same flophouse. The thief kills the owner of the flophouse and after a term in jail leaves with the owner's daughter. The Baron stays on amidst society's outcasts.

La Grande Illusion
(Grand Illusion, 1937)
Crew: *Director* Jean Renoir, *Producers* Frank Rollmer, Albert Pinkévitch, Alexandre, *Scenario* Charles Spaak, Jean Renoir, B&W, 113 minutes.
Cast: Jean Gabin (Maréchal), Pierre Fresnay (Boeldieu), Marcel Dalio (Rosenthal), Erich von Stroheim (Rauffenstein), Elsa (Dita Parlo).
French officers plot their escapes from a succession of First World War German prison camps. The film shows the camaraderie among soldiers of the same social class or occupation despite national barriers. Maréchal and Rosenthal eventually escape, thanks to the sacrifice of the upper-class Boeldieu. They spend Christmas Eve with a German farm wife and then cross over into Switzerland.

La Marseillaise *(1938)*
Crew: *Director* Jean Renoir, *Producers* André Zwobada, A. Seigneur, *Scenario* Jean Renoir, Carl Koch, B&W, 131 minutes.
Cast: Pierre Renoir (Louis XVI), Lise Delamare (Marie Antoinette), Edmond Ardisson & Charles Blavette (Bomier), Andrex (Arnaud), Nadia Sibirskaïa (Louison), Edouard Delmont (Cabri).
The film follows the fortunes of a battalion of volunteers from Marseilles, raised to support the Revolution. After a long march, and an introduction to Parisian customs, the battalion takes part in the storming of the Tuileries and the overthrow of the monarchy.

La Bête humaine *(The Human Beast, 1938)*
Crew: *Director* Jean Renoir, *Producer* Roland Tual *Scenario & Adaptation* Jean Renoir, Denise Leblond-Zola, B&W, 100 minutes.
Cast: Jean Gabin (Jacques Lantier), Simone Simon (Séverine), Fernand Ledoux (Roubaud), Carette (Pecqueux), Jean Renoir (Cabuche).
When Roubaud suspects that Séverine, his wife,

has been unfaithful, he forces her to help him kill the influential Grandmorin on the Paris-Le Havre express. They are observed by Jacques Lantier, who holds his tongue because of his passion for Séverine. However, overcome by an hereditary madness, he kills her and commits suicide.

La Règle du jeu
(The Rules of the Game, 1939)
Crew: *Director & Producer & Scenario* Jean Renoir, B&W, 106 minutes.
Cast: Roland Toutain (André Jurieux), Marcel Dalio (Robert), Nora Gregor (Christine), Jean Renoir (Octave), Paulette Dubost (Lisette), Mila Parely (Geneviève), Gaston Modot (Schumacher), Carette (Marceau).
After flying the Atlantic solo for Christine, André Jurieux blurts out his feelings on the radio and is heard by all of Paris. Robert, Christine's husband, invites André to his country estate where various love intrigues are played out during a hunt followed by a fête. Through a mistake in identity, André is killed by Schumacher, the gamekeeper, for which mishap Robert apologizes to his guests.

Swamp Water *(1941)*
Crew: *Director* Jean Renoir, *Producer* Irving Pichel, *Scenario* Dudley Nichols, B&W, 89 minutes.
Cast: Dana Andrews (Ben Ragan), Walter Brennan (Tom Keefer), Anne Baxter (Julie Keefer), Walter Huston (Thursday Ragan).
Ben Ragan goes into Okefenokee Swamp after his dog Trouble, only to stumble across the fugitive Tom Keefer who has been hiding out for a murder he did not commit. When Ben discovers the identity of the real murderers, he is able to lead Tom out of the swamp and return him to the community. Ben and Julie, Tom's daughter, are a couple.

This Land is Mine *(1943)*
Crew: *Director* Jean Renoir, *Producers* Jean Renoir, Dudley Nichols, *Scenario* Dudley Nichols, Jean Renoir, B&W, 103 minutes.
Cast: Charles Laughton (Albert Lory), Maureen O'Hara (Louise Martin), George Sanders (George Lambert), Walter Slezak (Major von Keller).
The Germans occupy a town "somewhere in Europe". When the schoolteacher Albert Lory is

wrongfully arrested for murder in a case related to a local saboteur, his mother tells the authorities who committed the sabotage. Albert is about to be freed, until he witnesses the execution of his school principal and decides to speak out against the Occupation.

Salute to France *(1944)*
Crew: *Directors* Jean Renoir, Garson Kanin, *Producer* Burgess Meredith, *Scenario* Philip Dunne, Jean Renoir, Burgess Meredith, B&W, 34 minutes.
Cast: Claude Dauphin (Jacques), Garson Kanin (Joe), Burgess Meredith (Tommy).
Three Allied soldiers on a troop ship bound for the liberation of France discuss the reasons for the Occupation and the Resistance. To prepare U.S. soldiers for the invasion, French daily life is illustrated with enactments by the three soldiers in civilian dress.

The Southerner *(1945)*
Crew: *Director* Jean Renoir, *Producers* David Loew, Robert Hakim, *Scenario & Adaptation* Hugo Butler, William Faulkner, B&W, 92 minutes.
Cast: Zachary Scott (Sam Tucker), Betty Field (Nona Tucker), J. Carroll Naish (Henry Devers), Charles Kemper (Tim), Norman Lloyd (Finley).
Sam Tucker decides to become a tenant farmer rather than work as a hired hand. He and Nona set out to make a home and clear land in hopes of raising a cotton crop, but meet with a succession of both human and natural disasters. Despite every setback, their resilience and faith in each other carries them through.

The Diary of a Chambermaid *(1946)*
Crew: *Director* Jean Renoir, *Producers* Benedict Bogeaus, Burgess Meredith, *Scenario &*

Adaptation Burgess Meredith, Jean Renoir, B&W, 86 minutes.
Cast: Paulette Goddard (Celestine), Francis Lederer (Joseph), Hurd Hatfield (George), Burgess Meredith (Mauger), Judith Anderson (Mrs. Lanlaire).
Celestine takes a position as chambermaid in the provincial Lanlaire household. Joseph, the valet, plans to abscond with the family's silver and to take Celestine with him. She is in love with George, but their relationship cannot be consummated until Joseph is killed by the townspeople during Bastille Day celebrations.

The Woman on the Beach *(1948)*
Crew: *Director* Jean Renoir, *Producer* Jack Gross, *Scenario & Adaptation* Frank Davis, Jean Renoir, Michael Hogan, B&W, 70 minutes.
Cast: Joan Bennett (Peggy Butler), Robert Ryan (Lt. Scott Burnett), Charles Bickford (Tod Butler), Nan Leslie (Eve Geddes).
A Coast Guard Lieutenant is troubled by wartime nightmares. He meets Peggy Butler and her husband, Tod, a blind painter, and falls in love with Peggy. The threesome can only be released from their troubled pasts when Tod sets fire to his remaining paintings.

The River *(1951)*
Crew: *Director* Jean Renoir, *Producer* Kenneth McEldowney, *Scenario & Adaptation* Rumer Godden, Jean Renoir, Technicolor, 99 minutes.
Cast: Patricia Walters (Harriet), Adrienne Corri (Valerie), Rhada Sri Ram (Melanie), Thomas Breen (Captain John), Richard Foster (Bogey).
Three adolescent, Westernized girls come of age in India. The film follows their troubled search for identity as they all learn to accept the fate that has been dealt them. Their lesson is learned against the backdrop of a Hindu culture whose life and ritual are a rich counterweight to European values.

The Golden Coach *(1953)*
Crew: *Director* Jean Renoir, *Producers* Francesco Alliata, Renzo Avanzo, *Scenario* Jean Renoir, Renzo Avanzo, Ginette Doynel, Jack Kirkland, Giulio Macchi, Technicolor, 103 minutes.
Cast: Anna Magnani (Camilla), Duncan Lamont (Ferdinand, the Viceroy), Paul Campbell (Felipe), Riccardo Rioli (Ramon, the bullfighter).
A commedia dell'arte troupe, led by Camilla, its star, arrives in colonial Peru at the same time as a magnificent golden coach. Three men are in love with Camilla: the Viceroy, Felipe and Ramon. She renounces all of them for the stage, along with the golden coach which the Viceroy had presented her as a gift.

French Cancan *(1955)*
Crew: *Director & Scenario* Jean Renoir, *Producer* Louis Wipf, Technicolor, 105 minutes.
Cast: Jean Gabin (Danglard), Françoise Arnoul (Nini), Maria Félix (la Belle Abbesse), Jean-Roger Caussimon (Baron Walter), Gianni Esposito (Prince Alexandre).
In 1889 the impresario Danglard builds a great Paris music-hall, the Moulin Rouge, with a new dance called the cancan as its most sensational attraction. Fortunes in love and money rise and fall parallel to the building of the Moulin Rouge, but the exhilaration of the dance heals all wounds.

Elena et les hommes
(Elena and Her Men, 1956)
Crew: *Director* Jean Renoir, *Producer* Louis Wipf, *Scenario* Jean Renoir, Jean Serge, Technicolor, 98 minutes.
Cast: Ingrid Bergman (Princess Elena), Jean Marais (General Rollan), Mel Ferrer (Henri de Chevincourt), Pierre Bertin (Martin-Michaud).
Elena is a Polish princess without means who endeavours to persuade General Rollan to take advantage of his popularity and stage a coup d'état. The General is more interested in affairs of the heart and runs away with his mistress, while Elena settles for the importunate Henri over the impossible Martin-Michaud.

Le Déjeuner sur l'herbe
(Picnic on the Grass, 1959)
Crew: *Director & Scenario* Jean Renoir, *Producer* Ginette Courtois-Doynel, Eastmancolor, 92 minutes.
Cast: Paul Meurisse (Etienne Alexis), Catherine Rouvel (Nénette), Fernand Sardou (Nino, her father), Ingrid Nordine (Marie-Charlotte), Charles Blavette (Gaspard).
Professor Etienne Alexis, a proponent of artificial insemination, is to be married to Marie-Charlotte, the German head of the European Girl Scout movement. Their union will represent the triumph of a new European state devoted to technology. When Alexis rekindles his repressed desires in the arms of Nénette, he decides that a marriage of science and nature will be more (re)productive.

Le Testament du Docteur Cordelier

(The Testament of Doctor Cordelier, 1959)
Crew: *Director & Scenario* Jean Renoir, *Producer* Albert Hollebeke, B&W, 95 minutes.
Cast: Jean-Louis Barrault (Cordelier/Opale), Teddy Bilis (Maître Joly), Michel Vitold (Dr. Séverin).
To be free from social constraint, the respected, if ascetic psychiatrist Dr. Cordelier experiments with a potion that transforms him into the violent, libidinous Opale. In the end, Opale takes a fatal dose of the potion and dies a suicide transformed once again as Cordelier.

Le Caporal épinglé

(The Elusive Corporal, 1962)
Crew: *Director* Jean Renoir, *Producer* G.W. Beyer, *Scenario & Adaptation* Jean Renoir, Guy Lefranc, B&W, 105 minutes.
Cast: Jean-Pierre Cassel (the Corporal), Claude Rich (Ballochet), Conny Froboess (Erika), Claude Brasseur (Papa).
The Corporal, a French prisoner under the terms of the Second World War armistice with Germany, makes many attempts at escape. He is only successful when he realizes that he must make a commitment to accept responsibility for his actions by continuing the fight against the German occupiers.

Le Petit théâtre de Jean Renoir

(The Little Theatre of Jean Renoir, 1969)
Crew: *Director & Scenario* Jean Renoir, *Producer* Robert Paillardon, Eastmancolor, 98 minutes.
Cast: 'Le Dernier Réveillon' ('The Last Christmas Eve'): Nino Formicola (the male tramp), Milly Monti (the female tramp); 'La Cireuse électrique' ('The Electric Floor Polisher'): Marguerite Cassan (Emilie), Pierre Olaf (Gustave); 'Quand l'amour meurt' ('When Love Dies'): Jeanne Moreau (the singer); 'Le Roi d'Yvetot' ('The King of Yvetot'): Fernand Sardou (Edmond), Françoise Arnoul (Isabelle), Jean Carmet (M. Féraud), Roger Prégor (Maître Joly).
Four sketches, each on a theme dear to Renoir over the course of his career, and each in a different style that draws on the tension between theatre and life: the inequities of social class; the horrors of technology; the fleetingness of passion; the futility of struggle.

Bibliography

Bibliographies

— Faulkner, Christopher: *Jean Renoir: A Guide to References and Resources*. G.K. Hall l979.
— Viry-Babel, Roger: *Jean Renoir: films/ textes/ références*. Presses Universitaires de Nancy. 1989.

Writings and Interviews

— Renoir, Jean: *Les Cahiers du Capitaine Georges*. Gallimard 1966. *The Notebooks of Captain Georges*. Collins 1966. Little, Brown 1966. *Il diario del capitano Georges*. Garzanti 1968. *Das intime Tagebuch des Capitaine Georges*. Dtv-Verlag 1970.
— Renoir, Jean: *Le Coeur à l'aise*. Flammarion 1978.
— Renoir, Jean: *Le Crime de l'anglais*. Flammarion 1979.
— Renoir, Jean: *Ecrits 1926-1971*. Editée par Claude Gauteur. Belfond 1974. Ramsay Poche 1989.
— Renoir, Jean: *Geneviève*. Flammarion 1980.
— Renoir, Jean: *Entretiens et propos*. Eds. de l'Etoile-Cahiers du Cinéma 1979. Ramsay Poche 1986.
— Renoir, Jean: *Letters*. Edited by David Thompson and Lorraine LoBianco. Faber and Faber, 1994. *Cõrrespondance 1913-1978*. Plon 1998.
— Renoir, Jean: *Le passé vivant*. Editée par Claude Gauteur. Eds. de l'Etoile-Cahiers du Cinéma 1989.
— Renoir, Jean: *Jean Renoirs Theater/Filme*. Redaktion Michael Lommel, Volker Roloff. Wilhelm Fink Verlag 2003.
— Renoir, Jean: *Julienne et son amour*. Présentation de Claude Gauteur. Henri Veyrier 1979.
— Renoir, Jean: *Lettres d'Amérique*. Présentées par Dido Renoir et Alexander Sesonske. Presses de la Renaissance, 1984.
— Renoir, Jean: *Ma Vie et mes films*. Flammarion 1974. *My Life and My Films*. Atheneum 1974. *Mein Leben und meine Filme*. Piper 1975. *Mi vida, mis films*. Valencia 1975.
— Renoir, Jean: *Oeuvres de cinéma inédites*. Réunis et présentés par Claude Gauteur. Cahiers du Cinéma - Gallimard, 1981.
— Renoir, Jean: *Orvet*. Gallimard 1955.
— Renoir, Jean: *Renoir*. Hachette, 1962. *Renoir, My Father*. Little, Brown 1962. *Mein Vater Auguste Renoir*. Piper 1962. *Renoir, mio padre*. Garzanti 1963.
— Renoir, Jean: *Renoir On Renoir*. Cambridge University Press 1989.

Screenplays

— 'La Chienne.' *L'Avant-Scène du cinéma* 62, 1965.
— Prévert, Jacques: *Le Crime de Monsieur Lange*. Gallimard, 1990.
— *Grand Illusion*. Lorrimer, 1968. Simon and Schuster, 1968.
— *La Grande Illusion*. Balland, 1974.
— 'Partie de campagne.' *L'Avant-Scène du cinéma* 21, 1962.
— Curchod, Olivier & Faulkner, Christopher (eds.): *La Règle du jeu: scénario original de Jean Renoir*. Nathan, 1999.
— Gassner, John & Nichols, Dudley (eds.): 'The Southerner.' *Best Film Plays - 1945*. Crown, 1946.
— 'Le Testament du Docteur Cordelier.' *L'Avant-Scène du cinéma* 6, 1961.
— *This Land is Mine*. Frederick Ungar, 1986.
— 'Toni.' *L'Avant-Scène du cinéma* 251-252, 1980.

Biographies, Books and Articles

— Andrew, Dudley: 'Jean Renoir: Adaptation, Institution, Auteur.' *Mists of Regret*. Princeton University Press, 1995.
— Bazin, André: *Jean Renoir*. Eds. Champs Libre, 1971. *Jean Renoir*. Simon and Schuster, 1973.
— Bergan, Ronald: *Jean Renoir: Projections of Paradise, A Biography*. Bloomsbury, 1992.
— Bergstrom, Janet: 'Jean Renoir's Return to France.' *Poetics Today* 17, 1996.
— Bertin, Célia: *Jean Renoir*. Perrin, 1986. *Jean Renoir: A Life in Pictures*. Johns Hopkins, 1991.
— Buchsbaum, Jonathan: '"My Nationality is Cinematography": Renoir and the National Question.' *Persistence of Vision* 12/13, 1996.
— Cavagnac, Guy: *Jean Renoir: le désir du monde*. Eds. Henri Berger, 1994.
— Chardère, Bernard (ed.): 'Jean Renoir.' *Premier Plan* 22-24, 1962.
— Curot, Frank (ed.): *Nouvelles approches de l'oeuvre de Jean Renoir*. Université Paul-Valéry Montpellier III, 1995.
— Curot, Frank: *Jean Renoir, l'eau et la terre*. Minard, 1990.
— De Costa, Joao Bernard (ed.): *Jean Renoir*. Cinemateca Portuguesa, 1994.
— De Vincenti, Giorgio: *Jean Renoir. La vita, i film*. Marsilio, 1996.
— Durgnat, Raymond: *Jean Renoir*. University of California Press, 1974.
— Faulkner, Christopher: 'An Archive of the (Political) Unconscious.' *Canadian Journal of Communication* 26, 2000.
— Faulkner, Christopher: 'Jean Renoir Addresses the League of American Writers.' *Film History* 8, 1996.
— Faulkner, Christopher: *The Social Cinema of Jean Renoir*. Princeton University Press, l986.
— Gassen, Heiner (ed.): 'Jean Renoir und die Dreissiger.' *Cicim* 42, 1995.
— Gauteur, Claude: *Jean Renoir: La Double méprise (1925-1939)*. Les Editeurs Français Réunis, 1980.
— Gilliatt, Penelope: *Jean Renoir: Essays, Conversations, Reviews*. McGraw-Hill, 1975.
— Gregor, Ulrich (ed.): *Jean Renoir und seine Film: eine Dokumentation*. Verband der deutschen Filmclubs, 1970.
— O'Shaughnessy, Martin: *Jean Renoir*. Manchester University Press, 2000.
— Quintana, Angel: *Jean Renoir*. Catedra, 1998.
— Serceau, Daniel: *Jean Renoir, l'insurgé*. Le Sycomore, 1981.
— Serceau, Daniel: *Jean Renoir, la sagesse du plaisir*. Eds. du Cerf, 1985.
— Sesonske, Alexander: *Jean Renoir: The French Films 1924-1939*. Harvard University Press, 1980.

Documentaries

— Bazin, Janine-André & Rivette, Jacques: *Jean Renoir vous parle de son art*. ORTF 1961.
— Bazin, Janine-André & Labarthe, André S.: *Renoir le patron*. ORTF 1967.
— Weldon, Huw: *Renoir on Renoir*. BBC Monitor Series 1962.

Websites

www.myweb.tiscali.co.uk/jeanrenoir
www.univ-nancy2.fr/renoir

Notes

1. Bakhtin, Mikhail: 'Forms of Time and the Chronotope in the Novel.' *The Dialogic Imagination*. University of Texas Press 1981.
2. Renoir, Jean: *My Life and My Films*. Atheneum 1974.
3. See note 2.
4. Renoir, Jean: 'Memories' in André Bazin: *Jean Renoir*. Simon and Schuster 1973.
5. See note 4.
6. See note 4.
7. Bazin, André: *Jean Renoir*. Simon and Schuster 1973.
8. See note 2.
9. Brooks, Peter: *Body Work*. Harvard University Press 1993.
10. Willard, James: 'Marquitta.' *Cinémagazine* 7, 1927.
11. Saffar, Paul: *Cinémagazine* 2, 1929.
12. See note 7.
13. Sadoul, Georges: 'A Masterpiece of Cinema: La Bête humaine' in Richard Abel (ed.): *French Film Theory and Criticism: Volume II, 1929-1939*. Princeton University Press 1988.
14. See note 2.
15. See note 2.
16. Renoir, Jean: 'How I Came to Film Boudu.' *Film Society Review* 1967.
17. See note 2.
18. See note 2.
19. See note 7.
20. See note 2.
21. See note 4. For the confrontation with Zanuck and the Baxter anecdote, see note 1.
22. Faulkner, Christopher: 'Jean Renoir Addresses the League of American Writers.' *Film History* 8, 1996; and, 'An Archive of the (Political) Unconscious.' *Canadian Journal of Communication* 26, 2000.
23. Sesonske, Alexander: 'The Amazing Mrs. Holliday.' *Films In Review* 38, 1987.
24. Sesonske, Alexander: 'Jean Renoir in America: 1942, This Land Is Mine.' *Persistence of Vision* 12/13, 1996.
25. See note 2.
26. See note 2.

Acknowledgements

This book is for Lila (with the hope that she will enjoy it in time). Thanks to Olivier Curchod and Claude Gauter for years of friendship and conversation about Renoir; Alain and Pat Renoir for many kindnesses; Nick Nguyen; Zuzana Pick; and all those students and colleagues over the years who have been good listeners. Especially my kids, Ursula, Graham, Jason and Gwen.

The editor would also like to thank Alain Renoir for giving his blessing to the project and allowing access to the Jean Renoir papers at UCLA, and to Janet Bergstrom for research materials.